LOOKING GOOD,
BEING BAD

LOOKING GOOD, BEING BAD

THE SUBTLE ART OF CHURCHMANSHIP

Adrian Plass

Authentic

First published 2009 by Authentic Media
Reprinted 2010, 2011 by Authentic Media Limited
52 Presley Way, Crownhill, Milton Keynes, MK8 0ES
www.authenticmedia.co.uk

British Library Cataloguing in Publication Data

A catalogue record for this book is available from the
British Library

ISBN 978-1-85078-898-0

Design and illustration by Anna Danby
Printed and bound by CPI Group (UK) Ltd, Croydon, CR0 4YY

To my friend Ian Peirce
who died before this book could be published.
He was transparently good, a trusty knight indeed.

CONTENTS

I would like to thank all the people who made suggestions for this book. They are too numerous to name specifically, and I would only forget someone. I should also express my appreciation of Stephen Potter's *Lifemanship* books, published in the late forties and early fifties. Fascinating and funny, they inspired the particular style of this book, and indeed much of the stuff I have produced over the last twenty years. I hope and suspect that Potter would agree with me when I say that there is nothing funny about humour. It has to be taken very seriously indeed, especially if you want to make people laugh and think at the same time. I hope you enjoy *Looking Good, Being Bad*. Turn it inside out and you will see just how much I love the church.

PROLOGUE

The whole thing was most peculiar. Spooky even.

Late one night my friend Jake was driving me down from Lancaster to Salisbury. Just south of Worcester we were both feeling drained with exhaustion and decided to pull over to the side of the A38 for a nap. When I awoke we were on the move again, but somewhere along the way Jake must have taken a wrong turning. I noticed a sign saying that we were heading for a place called Great Malvern. Jake was still yawning loudly, but he pulled over and stopped when I pointed out that we were probably going in the wrong direction.

'Let's ask,' he said. 'You ask. Go and ask someone.'

'That's all very well,' I complained, 'but who? Where? It's so late.'

'Try up that drive,' he said, cosying down in his seat and closing his eyes.

I did. The drive that Jake had indicated with a flick of his thumb curled away from the main road between ranks of magnificent horse chestnut trees, broadening into a wide, floodlit parking space in front of a Victorian red-brick house of impressive dimensions. Through the uncurtained window of a brightly illuminated room to the left of the front door, I could see a man working at a desk. I decided to chance it. Rapping rather nervously on the massive portico with my bare knuckles, I noticed a wooden frame at the side of the porch bearing the following legend:

SITUS USUSFRUCTUM ADDIT

My knowledge of Latin is nil, but later, as you will discover, I was to learn the meaning of these words.

The door was opened within a few seconds by a tall, handsome man, blonde-haired and dressed entirely in white. He delivered his greeting in suave, mellow tones.

'May I be of assistance? My name is Professor Peter Caws, and I am the principal of the College of Churchmanship here at Churchmanship Headquarters.'

I explained a little nervously that we were on our way to Salisbury and had missed a turning. We were now facing in the direction of Great Malvern.

'Simple,' he replied. 'Turn your car, go back through the villages of Bowling Green and Powick until you come to the roundabout. Turn right on to the A44, then right again at the next roundabout, and the A38 will take you south.'

'Thank you very much,' I responded, 'sorry to trouble you so late.' About to turn away, I paused. 'By the way, what is the – you know – the College of Churchmanship?'

The man raised an elegant eyebrow.

'We do not advertise ourselves unduly,' he said, 'but I would be happy to give you a copy of this year's annual report if it would interest you. The printers delivered them only this morning.'

He disappeared and returned a few seconds later with a thick, paper-backed volume.

'Take this with my compliments. Perhaps you would be interested in signing up for one of our courses.'

'I really dislike going on courses,' I said.

'Interesting. We have a two-week foundation course especially designed for those who dislike going on courses.'

'Yes, well, I must be – you know. Thank you again.'

Suddenly, unaccountably frightened, I turned and fled into the night and down the drive. I threw myself into the passenger seat of Jake's car, flinging the report into the back as I slammed the door shut. Following the professor's instructions we turned the car and set off in the direction of the roundabout that would put us back on track.

Soon after that I must have fallen into a deep sleep. I woke to find the car stationary and Jake asleep beside me. The extraordinary, baffling thing was that we seemed to be at exactly the same spot on the A38 where we had stopped for our nap in the first place. Impossible, surely.

Had it all been a dream? I supposed it must have been, but something prevented me from sharing the experience with Jake. In fact, I hardly said a word all the way to Salisbury. It was only when Jake dropped me off at home a couple of days later and called out, 'Don't forget your book!' that I realized, dream or not, Professor Caws' report had been lying on the floor of the car for the previous two days.

I've had a chance to read it now. You read it. It is a most extraordinary document. I have often wondered why progress seems to be such uphill work in the Christian church. Can it really be that there is an organized body of people whose express aim is to – well, you read the report and see what you think.

Incidentally, I did try to locate a telephone number or some other form of address for Churchmanship Headquarters, but I was unsuccessful. As you will see in the report, Professor Caws includes an address intended for the use of applicants to his Question and Answer section, but my letters have been returned and I am unable to verify that it exists. One day I might go back to Great Malvern and search for the horse chestnut avenue and the big house, but I have a more than sneaking suspicion that it will not be there.

Who is Peter Caws? I have no idea, but there is something about the name that troubles me. Something teasingly reminiscent of a different character altogether. I keep thinking I've got it, but then it slips away. I cannot quite remember . . .

—— LOOKING GOOD —— BEING BAD

THE SUBTLE ART
OF CHURCHMANSHIP

Annual Report for 2009
by Professor Peter Caws

It is a pleasure and a privilege for me as principal of the College of Churchmanship to present this report for 2009. The past year has seen our movement graced with so many new triumphs and fresh innovations that we are encouraged and confirmed in our assertion of the central tenets of Churchmanship. We continue to insist that a complete lack of faith or belief, and an unwillingness to contribute time, energy or money to any aspect of Christian living need never be a barrier to membership in and involvement with the church. However, we must always bear in mind that our art is intended to be a subtle and undiscovered one. In the pages of this special anniversary report we celebrate those from the present and the past who, by their example and expertise, are able to assist and educate us in this respect. I commend this report to you.

Section 1
PRAYERMANSHIP

──PRAYING FOR HEALINGMANSHIP──

I need hardly say how very proud we all are of the fine work that has been done in this area by past students of the college. I will not mention names as many of these folk are so well known now, and this report might fall into the wrong hands, but it is a great joy to see so many familiar faces and hairstyles at meetings and conferences, and on the television. Their signed photographs line the corridors here at Headquarters. It is a source of deep satisfaction that these great Churchmen and women continue to use the ploys and practices that were taught to them at Frome in days of yore, or, more recently, at our fine new building here in Great Malvern where our experts train students in the use of state-of-the-art concealed communication devices.

Take heart! That is my message to all involved in Praying for Healingmanship. Genuine healing ministries may come and go, but our operations in this section of the church seem to go from strength to strength. Churchmanship Headquarters continues to offer support, advice and practical assistance to students in the field. Take, for instance, the phenomenal success of one of our very latest innovations.

2x AA BATTERIES
NOT INCLUDED

Handy Healing Handwarmers

These cheekily titled aids to impressive prayer for healing are completely safe to use and virtually impossible for the outsider to detect. The set consists of a pair of battery-operated pocket handwarmers (*available from Churchmanship Headquarters, price fifteen pounds per set, including postage and packing – see illustration*) ideal for use in situations where those who seek healing are anticipating that the hands of the person praying for them will give off a strange warmth. The good news is that they will not be disappointed. Simply place both hands in the side pockets of your coat or jacket or handbag as you go through the what-can-I-do-for-you? chat before laying on hands, switch on the handwarmers and wait for two and a half minutes or until the palms of your hands are gently glowing with the heat. Repeat as necessary.

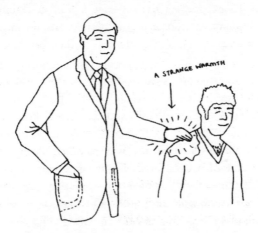

This is one of our most creative new ideas, and we are confident that this product will continue to simply fly off the shelves. If you haven't already, be sure to get your hands on a pair as soon as you can!

Begging Lettermanship

Churchmen and women must eat like everyone else, and the Churchman who takes up Healingmanship is no exception. His needs are just as great or greater (because naturally more hedonistic) than those of the man or woman who has a genuine healing ministry. To this end it is essential to grasp the basic principles of Begging Lettermanship, one of the easiest ways to ensure a steady flow of income throughout the year. We remind readers of the five main principles.

(1) Always ask for prayer above everything else

Make it clear very early on in your letter that prayer is the *first*, and money the *last*, thing on your list of requirements. Allow the need for cash to emerge or slip out accidentally, as it were.

> I have been called to minister God's healing power to the Matshawake tribe in the Carrabunda area of the Amazon Basin, and this will happen in September assuming that finances work out okay. Please pray for the suffering folk of Carrabunda that petty considerations concerning rent and transport in the intervening period will not stand in the way of their needs being met.

Make a point of enthusing with pathetic optimism about the severely limited resources that are available. This is vastly more productive in financial terms than complaint or self-pity.

> I never cease to marvel at the way in which all my needs are provided. Lots of reasons for giving thanks. Excitingly I have been able to heat one of the rooms in my house since a gift arrived in the post on Wednesday, and, marvel of marvels, I discovered a whole, unused candle in a drawer last week! Who needs electric light when miracles like this are happening every single month? God is in this. Forgive my childlike excitement, but I intend to save the candle up for a special occasion. How privileged I am to receive such bountiful provision!

Make a point of listing your own favourite charities and insist that people should give to these before they even think about financing you. In a stroke of genius, Prentice Basset of Streatham once offered to *send money to his own supporters* if they fell on hard times, explaining that although his resources were few he was determined that 'no one will go short if I can help it'. The money flowed in, and Basset ministered in Barbados that year.

(2) Keep it distant
If you are not planning to go anywhere at all make sure that most of your apparent destinations are in obscure parts of the world – countries so distant or inaccessible that nobody who reads your letter will ever be likely to go there. Include a smudgy little map in the bottom right-hand corner of the back page with a large arrow almost covering over a fuzzy-edged pink blob called 'Mandarak', located somewhere in the huge vagueness of Central Asia (*see illustration*). If anyone should express a desire to visit you on the mission field, simply arrange to have Mandarak overrun by a neighbouring state, or subjected to such a drastic natural disaster or pandemic that the cost of travelling there would be much better spent on relief, with the funds passing through your competent and capable hands.

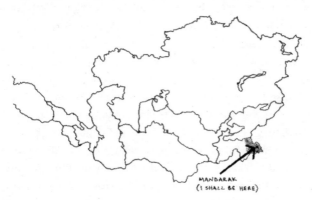

MANDARAK
(I SHALL BE HERE)

If you are planning to report a specific miracle, make sure that it happened in a small, crumbling hut halfway up a dangerously live volcano in some remote corner of Pakistan where there is no telephone and no possibility of sending or receiving e-mails.

(3) Always tell the truth about local events

If you feel it necessary to recount 'ministry' exploits nearer to home, always adhere strictly to the truth. Patrick Gift, graduate of this college, is a long-term expert in this area. Consider, for instance, this extract from his newsletter for July 2004.

> Something thrilling to share with all my partners and supporters. One Friday morning I received a phone call asking me to visit the house of a man already known slightly to me. It was clear not only to me but to everyone else involved in the situation that this man (I shall call him Mr Sefton) was going to die. I did all that Mr Sefton asked and expected of me and left, debating inwardly if I would ever see him again in this world. On the Saturday morning I received a second call to the same house. Arriving there I found Mr Sefton out of bed, fit and well and anxious to show me just how much could be done by a man with a strong body and a will to work. Praise God for what he has done in Mr Sefton's life!

A masterpiece. It was quite true that Gift was contacted that morning. The man called Sefton, who was not only superbly fit but had run his eighth three-hour marathon in that same year, was short of time and had some digging that needed to be done in his back garden. He was offering seven pound fifty an hour to anyone who would do it while he was at work. It was also true that Sefton was going to die. We all are. Gift did a bit of half-hearted poking at the earth, pocketed all the money that Sefton had misguidedly left on the kitchen table for him, and went home. It was entirely true that Gift might not have seen Sefton again in this world, but it was equally true that he might. And he did. The next day, when Sefton phoned again, Gift assumed there was more work on offer and went round, only to find that Sefton (out of bed because he gets up in the morning like everybody else, only with more alacrity because he is so hideously fit) was furious because only a tiny bit of the garden had been dug (badly) on the Friday. Sefton stood over Gift until the job was done properly and refused to pay him any more money.

One can only admire the way in which Gift turned a disaster into an advantage. Good Churchmanship often depends on creativity, and there is unanimous agreement here at Headquarters that Gift is full of it.

(4) Perfect the High-power Healing Posture and include illustration

Your letter should always prominently display a photograph of you, the healer, doing the business. Strict guidelines apply to the use of the *High-power Healing Posture (see illustration)*. May we remind you that, ideally, it should be executed as follows.

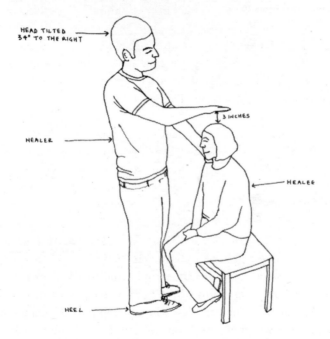

(a) Rest the left hand lightly but caringly on the right shoulder of the healee.
(b) Tilt the head to the right at an angle of thirty-four degrees.

(c) Adopt an expression of listening concentration, together with a small smile of confident intimacy, as though friendly instructions are being passed on from a different spiritual dimension.

(d) Raise the right arm until the end of the longest finger is three inches above the top of the head with the palm facing inwards and towards the left.

(e) A slight but very rapid bouncing motion on the heels may be indicated, but please be aware that the FGBMFI (Full Gospel Business Men's Fellowship International, in case you were wondering) has patents pending on this particular ploy.

(f) The photograph itself should be taken from the front, slightly left of the healee, with as many would-be healees queued up behind as possible.

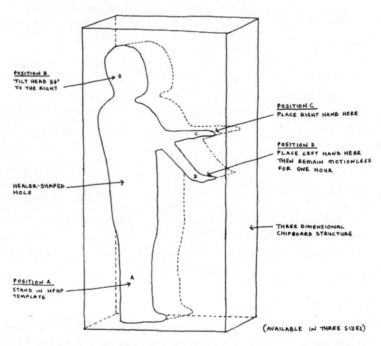

For those who are experiencing difficulties in successfully adopting the *High-power Healing Posture*, we are pleased to announce our brand-new product, the HPHP Template (*available from Churchmanship Headquarters, price twenty-four pounds per self-assembly template in mint green or distressed orange, including postage and packing – see illustration*). This slightly larger than life-sized model of a High-power Healer is constructed from especially hardened chipboard and allows the user to actually stand inside the figure, thus automatically conforming to the correct posture. Research indicates that an hour spent motionless inside the HPHP Template every day for one week will establish neural patterns that are not easily dispersed.

(5) *The little bit in biro at the bottom*

Always add a handwritten note at the bottom of the final page of your letter. The style should be one of informal intimacy, as though the person you are writing to is the only one in the world who really understands what you are going through. Patrick Gift provides a model for us all in this respect.

> *Hi, Chris, my old muckeroo! Sorry about sending you all the blurb and stuff. You of all people connect with what I'm doing without the need for loads of words, words, words… You've been there. I know that. I would only share this with you, my dear brother, heart to heart, but I'm in pain here, and it does me good just to know that you're standing with me in prayer as the work goes on. One day we'll meet and have some proper talk. That'll make my day, big-time!*

The truth was that Gift had met his 'old muckeroo Chris' once fleetingly at a promotional party but had somehow managed to drag contact details out of him before they parted. He received a cheque for a hundred pounds by return of post.

(6) *The turn away smile*

And finally, here's another useful tip from Patrick Gift and a bonus sixth point to add to our five basic principles. If you, the Churchman or woman, are called upon to pray for somebody's healing, it is good practice to conclude the prayer by turning quickly away from the prayee with a quiet but beatific smile of confidence on your face. The implication of this serene smile should be that you have fulfilled your duty to God and the suffering person to the very best of your ability, leaving the success or failure of your prayer totally dependent upon the inner response of the person who has been prayed for. To use Gift's own words:

> The skilled Churchman will never expose himself to the risk of taking responsibility for the outcome of any prayer that he has offered.

In this connection, we receive continual requests from members and students for guidance on how to deal with queries that arise from the (inevitable) non-healing that results from prayer by Churchmen and women. Gift suggests a number of sub-ploy responses. We include several of these below (*full list available from Churchmanship Headquarters, price two pounds including postage and packing*).[1]

(a) 'It depends what you mean by healing.' (*Say this with a coy, meaningful smile, but in the case of someone whose leg is hanging off select another response from the list below.*)

(b) 'It doesn't always happen immediately.' (*Yes, right . . .*)

(c) 'You will be more useful to God and other people in an unhealed state.' (*Really?*)

---

[1]   We are, incidentally, fully aware of the fact that many of these responses are not exclusively utilized by Churchmen and women, and they may even have some validity among the ranks of the sincere. That is not our concern and should never be allowed to distract us from the important work that lies ahead. We can do no better than to quote the great Vernon Poole on this very theme.

Allow the light of verity
To guide your insincerity
Thus may a clear and heartfelt lie
Be termed exactness by and by.

Surely nothing beyond these moving words remains to be said on the subject.

(d) 'There may be some sin in your life that needs sorting out.' (*The sin of extreme credulity perhaps.*)

(e) 'You lack sufficient faith.' (*You're Moses compared to the person who's praying for you.*)

(f) 'Death is the greatest healer of all.' (*Good news, eh?*)

(g) 'I wonder – do you really want to be healed?' (*Er, yes.*)

(h) 'You have been healed, but you need to claim your healing.' (*Interesting to note the continual success of this sub-ploy, despite its portrayal of healing as something you have to apply for like a prize in a Reader's Digest draw.*)

(i) 'There are some mysteries we are not allowed to understand.' (*Best emphasized by a sad shake of the head.*)

(j) 'God's reply to prayer can be "yes", "no", or "wait"'. (*God clearly opens the batting for some cricket team or other.*)

The Art of Speaking in Tongues

It is, of course, highly unlikely that any serious student of Churchmanship will genuinely speak in tongues, but for that very reason it is as well to be prepared. There are bound to be situations where the apparent use of this gift becomes strategically important. J.N. Vallant of Ipswich has supplied us with an invaluable aid to our efforts in this respect. Quite simply, all that is required is a copy of the Sri Lankan cricket team list from the early nineties. After exhaustive tests carried out here at Churchmanship Headquarters and in the field, we are pleased to report that Vallant's claims are entirely justified. Whether muttered in a dull monotone in the course of a prayer meeting or delivered boldly but with a slight slurring (obviously in the presence of those who have no knowledge of or interest in cricket), the repetition of these names is remarkably effective.

A colleague and acquaintance of mine actually had his recitation of the Sri Lankan cricket team interpreted by the lady next to him as a call from God to build a community launderette in the village of Cowfold in Sussex.

We include the list below for your use. Practice, as always, is helpful, and do bear in mind that, in vocal terms, a mystical dying fall or vocal twist is required at the conclusion of the final name.

Marvan Atapattu
Sanath Jayasuriya
Hashan Tillakaratne
Suresh Perera
Aravinda de Silva
Romesh Kaluwitharana
Pramodya Wickramasinge
Muthia Muralitharan
Kumara Dharmasena
Artuna Ranatunga
Mahela Jaywardena

A further word about the gift of Speaking in Tongues. There are two useful and contrasting stances for Churchmanship practitioners to take in this area, depending on the prevailing wind of opinion at the time and the place in which they find themselves.

First is the *Thank Goodness We've Got Away From All That* ploy, in which the Churchman or woman talks lightly and with an air of tolerant derision of the bad old days when charismatic churches were suggesting or insisting that genuine conversion is invariably accompanied by the gift of Speaking in Tongues. Point out that, in the twelfth chapter of the second book of Corinthians[2] Saint Paul asks the question, 'Do all speak in tongues?' Cite this as logical, incontrovertible evidence that the early church had no such foolish expectation. This ploy is particularly helpful in situations where a balanced, sensible interest in the spiritual gifts is developing and needs to be curbed.

If, on the other hand, you find yourself in a church setting where the general feeling is that folk are not yet ready or needing to prioritize gifts of this kind, use the *That Seems to Be What Happened Then* strategy, a sub-initiative, as we all know, of the *Don't Have a Go at Me I'm Only Quoting What the Bible Says* ploy. In this case say seriously and with an air of caring responsibility:

---

[2] This is one of those rare examples of a situation where it is strategically desirable for the Churchman or woman to take the trouble to learn words from the Bible and their exact reference.

Forgive me, but I really am only trying to understand what the Bible teaches us in this area. My question is this – can we read the first six chapters of the nineteenth chapter of the book of Acts and in good conscience continue to maintain that tongues or tongues and prophesy were not regarded as clear and common signs of authentic baptism at a time when patterns were being set for future Christian generations? It's only a question. 'When Paul placed his hands on them the Holy Spirit came on them and they spoke in tongues and prophesied.'[3] That's what my Bible says, and (*gravely*) I am bound to be faithful.'

---

[3] Another of those rare instances where it might be advisable to know some Scripture.

Section 2
EFFECTIVE
COMMUNICATIONMANSHIP

It is our unshakeable belief that almost any Churchman or woman, however joyously ignorant or splendidly indolent, is capable of speaking, writing or preaching on any biblical or spiritual subject so long as they learn and absorb the advice and instruction that is available from past and present masters of the art. Durham Steadman's fine if obscurely titled book *Sin Bull Hit* (*available from Churchmanship Headquarters, price fourteen pounds including postage and packing*) is, in our opinion, far and away the best reference book available. We begin this section with examples of points made by Steadman.

—————————— BE ORIGINAL ——————————

From time to time it may be strategically necessary for the Churchman or woman to deliver a talk or a piece of written work that is dull, stodgy and leadenly orthodox. The decline in sales of many of our Christian magazine publications is in itself a tribute to the unceasing efforts of little-known but dedicated graduates from the College of Churchmanship at Frome and latterly from Great Malvern. However, these unsung heroes would certainly agree that, in the main, our responsibility is to dazzle and disconcert with the originality of our approach to Scripture, books and historical figures, despite knowing almost nothing about them. This can be achieved in a variety of ways, but one of the most productive is to simply accuse any book, writer or famous Christian of failing to exhibit the very quality that has hitherto distinguished them.

A vivid example, and one that I have used to great advantage in talks and Bible studies, concerns the prophet Jonah. It was courage and loyalty, I unequivocally assert, that drove Jonah to take ship from Tarshish, and a blend of cowardice and sheer disobedience that finally caused him to preach in Nineveh. It was not so much that the great fish swallowed Jonah, I also comment in passing. Rather it was more that, in a very real sense, Jonah swallowed the great fish.

'Do we dare,' I enquire of the group or congregation I am addressing, 'to let ourselves look at the truth that lies behind a story that we *think* we know and understand, or will we hide behind bloodless convention, whispering miserably to God and each other that the truth does not interest us? My friends, hear you the challenge? And will you go?'

Usually they'll go all right, and quite honestly the biblical world and the Christian world in general is your oyster once you've got the hang of this. There are so many possibilities if you take the trouble to put a new spin on books of the Bible, historical figures and well-known writers. Examples from the Bible include:

- Acts: inaccessible and opaquely theoretical, not much sense of story or real-life action.
- Revelation: a nice break from those books that are difficult to fathom, probably the clearest and simplest one of all.
- Ecclesiastes: a great laugh written by a real optimist. Always cheers me up and reminds me that life is worth living after all. (I sometimes allow people to discover me chuckling away over Ecclesiastes, occasionally throwing my head back and coming out with a real belly laugh.)
- Psalms: no real sense of poetry or music. Tackles predominantly trivial issues and fails to plumb the depths of emotional need in those who yearn for God. Little awareness or acknowledgement of the dark side of human experience.
- Ruth: heavily laden with coarseness and brutality. Unsympathetic, loveless central characters who make the reader despair for humanity in general and women in particular.
- Genesis: leaves the reader with a deep desire to know more about the beginnings, the origins of creation, the early friendship between

God and his people, and what it was that destroyed the serenity of that relationship.
- Lamentations: too jolly.
- Philemon: too long.
- Isaiah: too short.
- Numbers: too distractingly emotional.
- Job: prosaic in style and a depressing reminder that men and women who go wrong through their own deliberate fault are very often unwilling to listen to the excellent advice of wise friends.
- Song of Songs: a passionless treatise on the intellectual and practical issues arising from formal interaction between men and women. Oh, for an acknowledgement of the sensual, sexual aspects of human relationships.
- James: a reminder that the way we behave and the things we do are of very little importance in comparison with our faith

Employ exactly the same intellectual exercise with historical figures:

- Martin Luther: a theological conformist lacking any sense of spiritual innovation.
- John Wesley: a man whose life and ministry was characterized and possibly diminished by his testy refusal to travel and teach because he missed his wife so much when he was away.
- Julian of Norwich: an East Anglian who was so busy fussing and fiddling with day-to-day stuff that she never got round to exploring the more abstract, mystical aspects of faith.
- Sir Thomas More: statesman and writer whose life and death serve as a stark reminder of the negative consequences that may result from the abandonment of our principles.
- General Booth: a flippant, frivolous man who, if he had not been so busy looking for opportunities to play practical jokes on all and sundry, might have done a great deal to benefit the physical and spiritual needs of the ordinary working man
- Padre Pio: a bit of a show-off. 'Look at me, everybody! I've got the stigmata. Have you? Don't *think* so!'

And then, of course, there are the Christian writers:

- C.S. Lewis: unimaginative and lacking in ingenuity. The writings of this man would have been improved by a greater depth of scholarship and philosophic intuition. What readers really want and need is to be taken into a new and different kind of world.
- Aiden Wilson Tozer: could have done with being rather more stern and a little less conciliatory. Does the cross really not matter?
- Gerard Manley Hopkins: where is the whimsy?
- Gilbert Keith Chesterton: where is the paradox?
- William Barclay: where are the Bible study notes?
- Saint Augustine of Hippo: all very well to preach about changing our lives and seeking redemption, but we might have been a little more willing to listen if Augustine had opened up about his own early life. Did he have a concubine, for instance, or any illegitimate children? Are we allowed to know?
- Saint Paul: educationally subnormal and lacking the true epistolary spirit, it might be thought that this poorly motivated serial doubter allowed his lack of confidence to create unnecessary barriers between Gentiles and the Gospel that they so needed to hear.

———— DISCOVER PROBLEMS WHERE ———— THERE ARE NONE

Hovering strangely between fear and appetite, there is a sense or instinct in many Christians that evil lurks in the most unexpected nooks and crannies of everyday life, waiting to ambush and attack the unwary believer. Churchmen and women who wish to influence others through speaking or writing should be aware of this proclivity and, from time to time, allow it to inform the work that they do. I offer as a sample extracts from a magazine article which I wrote for the 2001 spring issue of *Christian Alpha Families of the*

21st Century. It provoked over one hundred letters of gratitude, and, I would modestly suggest, probably ensured that the countryside was significantly less littered with Christian people for the whole of that season.

'HEY NONINO' OR 'NO-NO-NO!'

Durham Steadman investigates the hidden perils of a simple springtime stroll

You are out for a gentle walk, revelling in one of those wonderful spring days that we all love so much. The sky is blue, the sun is beaming, and little lambs are frisking in the fields beside their mothers. Flowers of blue and yellow and white, sensing that the long cold winter is over at last, tentatively open their trusting faces to receive and enjoy the warmth of April sunshine. The whole of creation seems to rejoice in the newness of life that is everywhere. What could be more innocent and pure than a stroll in the countryside at springtime? Surely there is nothing here to trouble the unwary believer – or is there?

Hurry Past

All of a sudden your eye is caught by green foliage spread across a patch of ground beside the footpath. You kneel to take a closer look, intrigued by the little heart-shaped leaves arranged in threes on their fragile stalks. This is the leguminous fodder plant of the genus *Trifolium*, commonly known as 'clover', and certainly known to Satan as a subtle means of drawing believers into sin. Is that a rare four-leaved example you suddenly spot over there just beyond the reach of your hand, a pagan symbol of good fortune? What if it is? Our trust does not repose in shallow superstition, though the devil will always seek to turn our heads with such temptations. Withdraw your hand, and hurry past the clover patch in future if you truly wish to honour God.

Skies of Grey

But, you ask, surely there can be no harm in relishing the serenity of a cloudless, eggshell-blue sky as I continue my walk?

Friend, this may seem to be the case, but surely the Lord would have us recall that there are many brothers and sisters who, because of depression or despair, see nothing but skies of grey overshadowing the bleak horizons of their lives? Would you so easily forget those suffering ones for the sake of your own pleasure? Eyes of flesh may see blue skies, but, as a matter of submission and identification, let the eyes of your spirit see black, lowering clouds filling the skies and threatening the land with storm and hail and lashing rain. Experience the true joy of obedience.

Occult Shapes

Well, you might wish to say to me, I am willing to be obedient in these matters, but surely there is nothing wrong with strolling quietly along looking at trees and fields and creatures, both wild and domestic, that I pass?

My reply to you is in the form of a question. Is Scripture to have no impact at all on the way in which we live our lives? In the twenty-second chapter of the second book of Kings we read that the eight-year-old king Josiah 'did what was right in the eyes of the Lord and walked in all the ways of his father David, not turning aside to the right or to the left'.

And of course that is how we must walk. Brothers and sisters, if you were to turn and look to the right or the left as you walk through the countryside you would understand the wisdom of this Scripture. There will be tree branches twisted into tortured occult shapes, cattle horned like the devil himself, rabbits that are possessed by the very spirit of fornication, budding fruits that will eventually symbolize the dripping juice of seduction and sin, and combine harvesters, their very name an unholy reminder that many are now yoked with churches that, unlike us, are believers in name only.

Five Helpful Points to Bear in Mind if You Are Planning a Springtime Stroll

(1) Never risk taking country walks on your own. It is much easier to combat evil and temptation if you are accompanied by a like-minded friend.

(2) Do not set out with the intention of gaining any personal satisfaction from your walk. Give the whole exercise to God before setting off and let him decide how it will be best used.

(3) Avoid looking at anything. What is the point in asking for trouble? Stare straight ahead and pray that you will be protected from all that is around you. Why not decide that you and your friend will take turns walking along with your eyes closed?

(4) Do not be tempted to slavishly use a map or route finder. The Lord is our guide, and he will ensure that we arrive at the destination he has planned for us. However late and dark it becomes, and however lost and hungry and bewildered we may feel, depend on it that these are lies sent to discourage us, and if we are faithful we shall end up in exactly the place where God wants us to be.

(5) Don't forget to enjoy it!

——— WRITING CHRISTIAN BOOKS ———

It is important to realize that, from the point of view of the Churchman or woman, only three aspects of any Christian book are of significance or interest. These are the front cover, the back cover and the opening two or three paragraphs. The actual content, which can be knocked off at the last moment after the real work on the first three items has been done, is of little relevance. Many Christian writers who know nothing of formal Churchmanship spend their time reinventing the wheel, as it were. Bearing this in mind,

Churchmen and women will readily understand how essential it is for readers to be protected from the realization that they are about to read the same book for the fifth or sixth time, albeit in a slightly different form.

The front cover, and the title in particular, should promise to solve a problem that is famously insoluble. My most successful book to date bore an arresting title in slightly raised, jet-black capital letters on a white background.

DESTROYING DOUBT

HOW TO ACHIEVE TOTAL, UNSWERVING FAITH IN LESS THAN SIX WEEKS

The front cover also included a powerful encouragement to potential readers:

'A life-changing book . . .'

I selected this useful legend (before the book was written, of course) from a stock of universal front-cover phrases that I have compiled over the years (*full list available from Churchmanship Headquarters, price three pounds including postage and packing*). It is essential to include the three full stops at the end of the phrase in order to imply, as they do, that this is just a tiny extract from a much longer and even more fulsome list of compliments by someone or other. Other front-cover options include:

'A gargantuan step forward for the entire Christian church . . .'

'Blinding light for those who live in darkness . . .'

'An extraordinary/staggering/astonishing/massive achievement . . .'

'A message straight from heaven . . .'

'Words of life, healing and inspiration . . .'

'A book that will literally move the earth off its axis . . .'

'The final answer to all things spiritual . . .'

'God himself wrote this book . . .'

The back cover should include a summary of the book's contents, usually known as the 'blurb', and glowingly positive comments from people (preferably well known) who may (or may not) have received a copy of the manuscript to read before it is published.

The blurb, as with the contents of the front cover, can be written before the book itself. *Destroying Doubt* was described (by me) in this manner.

> In this book Durham Steadman sets out to excavate and thoroughly explore an area of faith that has been neglected or indifferently dealt with in the past. Other books on the same subject ask questions. Steadman fearlessly provides the answers. In a series of easy to understand sections, every aspect of the problem is faced and dealt with in a way that will bring peace to the troubled soul and fulfilment to the yearning heart.[4]

Recommendations from famous people are a little trickier. In my own case, for instance, the response to manuscripts sent out by my publishers has been so uniformly negative that I have had to do a little creative editing in order to achieve the desired result. Here is

---

[4]   It is worth noting that these words can be used to describe almost any Christian book. I used them myself for the back cover of my subsequent book *Doubting Destruction*, for the third in the series *The Truth about Destruction and Doubt*, and also for the fourth, *Doubt and Destruction – The Interface*.

a copy of the original review from which I abstracted comments for the back cover of *Destroying Doubt*. I have highlighted in bold type the portions that finally appeared on the back of the book.

Not only is this an appallingly written book, but when I took the manuscript out of its envelope it was covered in some horrible, jam-like substance. After picking up the first page **I couldn't put it down** because it stuck to my fingers. This, coupled with the nauseous and inept sentiments expressed in the book, did terrible things to my whole system, **in fact I was up all night with it.** I should add that I particularly object to you, the publisher, suggesting to me in your accompanying letter that **Steadman is a rare Christian genius.** I prefer to make my own mind up about such things. I am not sure what the opposite of 'genius' is, but Steadman is one of them, whatever they are. By a huge effort of the will and purely as a matter of duty I actually managed to finish this dreadful book. **What an achievement!** It is absolute *garbage!* I found myself becoming increasingly agitated as I fought my way through the negative sludge of this horrible book. So disturbed was I that, in the end, I dumped every page of the manuscript on the fire, and **with Steadman's words blazing in my heart**h I **was able to find peace at last.** Please note that I do not wish to review any more books by the incompetent charlatans who write for your firm. This is my final letter to you, and **I shall be sending copies to all my friends**, warning them to have nothing to do with a publisher who sees no problem with producing **such an incredible outpouring** of utter drivel.

–Alec Delve, Maidstone

The final consideration is a strong, seductive first paragraph or two to catch the eye of the prospective reader. *Destroying Doubt* began like this:

From the vast golden bowl of the sky, a merciless sun beat down on the metal railway tracks to which my wrists and ankles were tightly lashed. Jeering and whooping, the fierce Aswari tribesmen had ridden their camels away into the eternal unforgiving desert, leaving me abandoned and alone. Now the long silence that had fallen after their departure was broken by the rush and roar of a mighty steam engine powering inexorably through the thin desert air in my direction. There would be no question of this metal giant stopping in time, even if the *Gobadi* or driver was sufficiently alert to spot my helpless body through the quivering haze. I called out desperately, but my feeble words were blown to shreds by the thunder of the monster's approach. All that stood between me and certain death was my faith in a God who can do miracles.

'Help me!' I cried hoarsely, my throat parched by the moistureless air. 'Help me, God!'

Less than thirty yards away now, the sooty behemoth pursued its roaring course along the single line track. I closed my eyes tight shut and waited for instant oblivion. Surely, nothing could save me now . . .[5]

I had first travelled to the centre of the Gobi desert as one member of a mission team whose aim was to translate and distribute etc., etc.

That's the sort of thing you need. Obviously you must write the rest of the content. It may seem a tiresome chore, but a certain number of pages have to be filled before the finished thing can reasonably be termed a 'book'. Any old stuff will do, though. Just get it down and send it off. As long as you've got the covers and the first few paragraphs right you'll be fine.

---

[5] Remember to reveal the end of your opening story at some point in the book, however sketchily. In this case I used an old fail-safe. The whole thing turned out to be a strange but meaningful dream. Most of my more sensational stories do.

── CHURCHMANSHIP AND POETRY ──

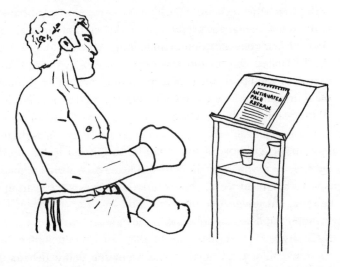

Our thanks to Steadman for those points. As far as I know that great Churchman has never attempted poetry, but in the early eighties Jerome Sandman, who trained in Creative Churchmanship at our old headquarters in Frome, made quite a name for himself as a poet at church events and festivals. The poetry that he wrote and recited was, by his own private admission, randomly assembled and entirely devoid of meaning, but there was something ineffably, shockingly bizarre about his habit of performing in boxing shorts and gloves and adjusting his make-up and hairstyle to look as much as possible like Joe Bugner, the one-time British heavyweight champion (*see illustration*). In addition, the style of his delivery was so intense and darkly meaningful that Christian audiences were transfixed, and in some cases greatly moved, by his offerings. Here is one example of his work. It is entitled 'Antiquated Pale Refrain'.

> Antiquated pale refrain
> You swallowed blue-infested pain
> And fenced around the Bunter cry

That twice evacuated lie
From some pearl-studded Belgian field
Where sad albino children wield
The wands of planetary light
In cold, exploding crimson night
I fear the rain, the hawthorn trees
The crumbled parks the poisoned seas
And how shall angels share their stars
With ravens in suburban bars?

I have it on the authority of Sandman himself, and I see no reason
to doubt his claim, that this ludicrous collection of words regularly
reduced audiences to tears. One woman said that, after hearing it,
she had properly understood predestination and free will for the first
time. Another donated a pool table to the Sailors' Society.

One style of Christian poetry that can be attempted and
mastered by almost any Churchman or woman is that known as the
List Of Opposites or, more familiarly, LOO. All that is needed here
is for each line to contain opposites in one form or another. It can be
quite short or as long as you wish. Elaine Broadwater of Haywards
Heath, who performs her popular works to Christians in her own
town and throughout the East Sussex area, has kindly allowed us to
quote the poem 'God Is' from her collection entitled *Poems From Up,
Down, Here, There, Everywhere and Nowhere. (Available from Churchmanship
Headquarters, price eight pounds fifty per volume, including postage and packing —
see illustration.)*

God is the soft heart of granite
The cold centre of fire
He is the past that is the future
The truth within the liar.
God is the wisdom of the foolish
The stillness of the tide
The summer in the winter
The humble face of pride

God is the dawn that breaks at nightfall
The smile behind the frown
The mountain in the valley
The pathway up from down.
God is the storm that wraps the stillness
The star in empty skies
The voice that breaks the silence
The life that never dies
God is the rain that floods the desert
The freely offered cost
The bird that flies where no birds fly
The finding of the lost.

Before finally deciding to publish 'God Is' in this report, I phoned Elaine and tentatively (the last thing I wanted to do was insult her) put it to her that the poem was perhaps a little too far along the road to being genuinely good. Should it be included in a report that would be read exclusively by Churchmen and women who are, quite rightly, more concerned with effect than substance? Elaine laughed heartily and pointed out that the 'poem' as it stands took her about half an hour to write.

'I could have gone on for ever,' she said. 'Black, white, short, tall, shallow, deep, love, hate, just bung 'em all together in a more or less reasonable order with a few rhymes thrown in and bob's your auntie! One poem, available for public, the reading to thereof. LOO is a piece of cake. Everyone should have a go.'

PULPY WORDMANSHIP

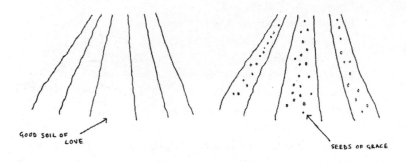

GOOD SOIL OF LOVE

SEEDS OF GRACE

Churchmen and women who are interested in Communication-manship have always been greatly aided in the preparation of their talks and presentations by the substantial number of 'pulpy' words that are common currency in the world of Christian communication. Other practitioners have demonstrated that this is certainly the case in the area of chorus and hymn lyrics, but, as we shall see, a much wider application is possible. The words we are dealing with here, though probably very significant in themselves, can become slack in meaning and virtually interchangeable when employed by experienced students of Churchmanship. Some of the most useful examples, first published in last year's report, are listed below.

Grace
Love
Obedience
Faith
Truth
Hope
Courage
Reverence
Humility
Peace

RAIN OF
OBEDIENCE

HARVEST OF
FAITH

The remarkably flexible nature of these terms can be vividly illustrated by a careful study of variations in sentences like this:

> If we plant the seeds of *grace* in the good soil of *love* and water them with the fresh rain of *obedience* we shall eventually reap the rich harvest of *faith*.

Extensive and well-documented experimentation suggests that the vast majority of groups and congregations will accept this frankly meaningless statement without question, especially when accompanied by a simple diagrammatic illustration (*see diagrammatic illustration*). After all, it contains a heavy sprinkling of words that are generally agreed to be 'okay', and it appears to make as much sense as most of the stuff they are accustomed to hearing. The fact is, though, that the order in which the key words are used has little or no effect on the general impact of the sentence. One might, for instance, decide to reverse them:

> If we plant the seeds of *faith* in the good soil of *obedience* and water them with the fresh rain of *love* we shall eventually reap the rich harvest of *grace*.

Similarly, chucking out a couple of words and filling the gaps with a pair of random replacements from the 'pulpy' list will make no difference at all, other than (crucially) allowing the Churchman or woman to truthfully claim that something new is being propounded:

> If we plant the seeds of *faith* in the good soil of *humility* and water them with the fresh rain of *hope* we shall eventually reap the rich harvest of *grace*.

Well, of course we shall. And even when all four words are replaced this pool of verbal opacity will remain as still and untroubled as a sheet of dark glass. Witness our final example:

> If we plant the seeds of *truth* in the good soil of *reverence* and water them with the fresh rain of *courage* we shall eventually reap the rich harvest of *peace*.

Profundity on a plate. And, properly used, a valuable substitute for time-consuming creative effort in the busy life of the Churchman.

It may be worth adding that Victor Stone of Newmarket reports using *all ten* of the words from our list in one sentence. He received, he tells us, not only a great deal of solemn nodding and murmured verbal assent in response, but also an actual round of applause. Spoken aloud by Stone, who counted off each key word on his fingers as though he was painstakingly working through a complicated but deeply interesting mathematical problem, the sentence took this form:

> When *grace* and *love* are confirmed by *obedience*, we find that *faith* embraces *truth*, thus allowing *hope* and *courage* to develop the *reverence* that leads to *humility* and will finally achieve *peace*.

Very good work by Stone, and even in a sentence as lengthy as this one we see that, once again, the key words are virtually interchangeable and, as you will observe, eminently reversible:

> When *peace* and *humility* are confirmed by *reverence*, we find that *courage* embraces *hope*, thus allowing *truth* and *faith* to develop the *obedience* that leads to *love* and will finally achieve *grace*.

By our current calculations, ten thousand million (10^9) permutations of this one sentence are possible – that's something new every morning for about 30 million years.

———————NEW WORDMANSHIP———————

It was Victor Stone who pointed out that the invention of *new* words for use in church circles might be equated to the practice of judo, that sport where the weight of one's opponent and the force of their attack is used to defeat them. Stone's meaning, profound to the point of discomfort in a true Churchman, is that there is already a tendency in the modern church to corral or contain religious and even normal behaviours into sub-cultural verbal capsules. Thus we are likely to hear, and indeed have heard, worship leaders announce that God will shortly be *'Presencing'* himself in the service.

Stone has assembled his own list of similarly novel words, and these are now available for the use of members *(full list available from Churchmanship Headquarters, price two pounds including postage and packing)*. Victor Stone makes the point that the introduction of these fresh terms into the vocabulary of any church community must be done unapologetically and with complete confidence. Ideally, the congregation should feel that, in the area of spiritual expression, they are the ones who are lagging behind whilst the Churchman or woman is simply employing terms that are common parlance in one of those big London churches where all the new movements and stuff seem to begin.

Stone's suggestions, helpfully placed in their appropriate con-texts, include these examples, and are best expressed in the floridly emboldened tones of modern worship leaders:

> The Lord is calling on those who are not in church every week to *abundantize* their *attendivity*.

> This morning we shall be celebrating the Lord's *renewalescence* of his people.

Lord, we pray for *ongoingness* in the *pentecostalment* of your church.

We bow our heads and move into a time of *confessance.* Let us come before God and confidently ask him to endorse our *absolvability.*

Let us test if the *inhabitingness* of praise will bring forth an *infillage* of joy.

———— THE POWER OF CONFIDENCE ————

Confidence is so important. Darley Jameson, a truly great Church-man of the past, strongly maintained that almost any statement or view will be accepted by a church audience or congregation as long as it is proclaimed with sufficient assurance. When I was a young man he told me that he had two distinctly different talks that he used whenever he was asked to preach on the book of Revelation. The opening sentences of these talks, he explained, needed to be delivered with a declamatory, faintly irritable intensity that indicated hard-won theological and intellectual battles of the past and excluded any possibility of disagreement. The first began with these words.

> The book of Revelation is *not* about judgement, and please do not allow yourselves to be led astray by those who, for their own very questionable reasons, wish you to believe that it is.

The second talk started with these words.

> The book of Revelation is *entirely* about judgement, and please do not allow yourselves to be led astray by those who, for their own very questionable reasons, wish you to believe that it is not.

After that, Jameson said, his listeners were as good as gold, happy in the belief that at last they were listening to someone who knew what he was talking about and would not be diverted from the truth by the machinations of this vague but ominous body of people who spend their time trying, for their own very questionable reasons, to lead everyone astray. Jameson's approach here is a stock-in-trade for the busy Churchman. There are few better ways of establishing one's point than to create an imaginary army of deluded, malicious or stupid people who hold the opposite view to you, and then to demolish them with righteous criticism. The sentence below, suggested by Jameson himself, is almost universally applicable. Simply fill in the end of the sentence with the opposite view to the one you wish to propagate:

Be aware and be wary, because people will undoubtedly try to tell you that . . .

Jameson's assertion about the value of the confidently expressed statement is borne out by Churchmen and women of all ages and levels of experience. My own Uncle Dexter Caplin, now in his early eighties and still happily disrupting a small church in Dartford on a part-time basis, offers very useful advice.

'I always think of the marriage service (Uncle Dex says), and the section where the minister says, "Those whom God has joined together, let no man put asunder". That is exactly the tone that needs to be injected into the statement that we are talking about. Take this sentence as an example:

Quite frankly, I don't *have* a quiet time.

Said with the right blend of bravura and righteous defiance it is possible to imply that, in this area, great issues have already been resolved and vast questions answered. The speaker, it seems to suggest, has moved on to some other, more rarefied dimension of spirituality that cannot be comprehended by those who are still weighed down by the leaden requirements of daily prayer and Bible study.

Here are some forms of words with which I have achieved great success in the past. My day is almost done, but it is my fond hope that a new generation of Churchmen and women will take the baton from me (strategically dropping it from time to time, of course).

(a) "I have to tell you with deeply mixed feelings of pungent sadness and, yes, with a strange species of trembling joy, that I can no longer support Third World[6] projects." (*Totally inexplicable but powerful, this ridiculous statement has the incredible effect of suggesting that, by not supporting Third World projects, I am being more responsible and obedient than if I do!*)

(b) "I for one refuse to do any more 'reaching out' until we have truly understood what it means to reach in." (*Remarkably powerful and apparently very deep, but either leave before questions can be asked or greet them with a sad, dignified silence – as though the triviality of the question is an insult to the profundity of the concept.*)

(c) "Okay, we can either grapple with the living, breathing Word of God, or we can turn this into a Greek lesson for beginners. I know you will forgive me[7] if I say that I know where my heart lies." (*Handy when someone has proved you wrong by referring to the original meaning of the text. Always bear in mind, though, that in some other context you may need to talk passionately about "a dangerously naive view of Scripture that is too frightened to use the tools of knowledge and intellect with which God has gifted us". Horses for courses, as they say.*)

(d) "I will not turn the Bible/church/minister/prayer/outreach/ social care/giving/fellowship into the third person of the Trinity. I simply will not do that!" (*Select or fill in as required with anything or anyone that is acquiring more importance or significance than is good for you personally Delivery should fall somewhere between Billy Graham and Martin Luther King. Guaranteed to stop, or at the very least postpone, the rot.*)'

---

[6] Churchmen and women should be deeply grateful to the Third World. In almost every conceivable situation points can be scored and undesirable directions altered by the use of one simple sentence. 'What does all this mean when we set it against chronic poverty and sickness in the Third World?' A winner every time.

[7] Note Uncle Dexter's instinctive use of *Aggressive Apology*. See section on this subject, below.

THE DUMPING YOUR TALK PLOY

Churchmen or women who have forgotten or neglected to prepare a talk or sermon will be keen to utilize this highly effective ploy, not least because they will be seen in a better light than if they had assiduously planned every word. Execution is brilliantly simple.

When the time comes for your talk to begin, take a thick sheaf of notes up to the lectern and, after laying it down, flick briefly through the pages as though you are doing a final check that they are all present and in order. After bowing your head and apparently saying a silent prayer, raise your eyes and gaze at the congregation with an expression of troubled inspiration (*see illustration*). Using one hand to pick up your notes and lay them to one side, use the other to raise a Bible to chest height and address the congregation with these or similar words in tones that, though measured, are clearly concealing a spiritually-fuelled zeal.

Good morning, everybody. You are here. I am here. My sermon (*talk/message/homily/address*) is over there (*indicate abandoned sheaf of notes*). The address (*homily/message/talk/sermon*) that I spent so many hours preparing for you this week may be a very good one. It may possibly be an extremely bad one. I suppose it is most likely to be a very average one. Be that as it may, you and I are not the only ones who are in this church (*school/chapel/sitting-room/ field/hall/converted factory*) this morning. God is also here, and I am bound to tell you, dear friends, that I believe he is telling me, even as I stand before you now, that the homily (*message/talk/sermon/ address*) I have brought with me (*indicate sheaf once more*) does not embody the lessons that he wishes to teach to us this morning. He would have me put it aside and read to you one of the most moving, poetic and – yes – challenging chapters in the whole of the New Testament.[8] Paul's first epistle to the Corinthians, chapter thirteen, beginning to read at verse one. (*Commence reading in thrilling, solemn tones with a hint of sad sweetness.*)

'If I speak in the tongues of men and of angels, but have not love, I am only a resounding gong or a clanging cymbal, etc. . .'

Having completed the reading, close your Bible with approp-riate gravitas, enfold it and the sheaf of notes in your arms, reverentially folded across your chest, and make your way with bowed head slowly back to a seat in the body of the church.

The benefits of this ploy are multi-layered. Not only has the Churchman been brave and obedient enough to lay aside a talk that took many hours to prepare, but he is also so spiritually sensitive that

---

[8] Mostyn Deal (*see section on Unsigned Greeting Cardmanship*) once spent a fortnight learning the whole of this chapter word for word before employing the Dumping Your Talk Ploy at his church on the next Sunday morning that he was due to speak. 'Afterwards,' reports Mostyn, 'when people told me how wonderful it had been, I looked slightly dazed and puzzled and said that I had no recollection of it happening at all, laughing at the very notion that I might know such a lengthy piece of Scripture by heart. After that there wasn't a lot to choose between Isaiah and Mostyn Deal. I think I might have just edged it.'

he is able to discern exactly what God wanted to say to this group of people on this particular morning. A fine result.

We at Churchmanship Headquarters are, of course, aware of the need for authenticity in these matters, and to that end we have produced our own sets of (apparently) handwritten talks in appropriately creased, crossed-out and footnoted sheaves of various thicknesses. The list of available titles includes:

Advance and retreat in the Pentateuch: An overview

Malachi: The relationship between promise and contention

The restoration of spiritual consistency: A contraction of Zephaniah

Clouds, climaxes and reconstitution: The heart of 2 Chronicles chapter five

Emission and retention: The real message of John 3:16

Intimations of purity: Purpose and peacemakers in the first two gospels

All titles are specially designed to suggest content that has resulted from vigorous intellectual research and passionate engagement with Scripture, and are now available for purchase from Headquarters (*priced from twelve pounds, fifty pence per sheaf including postage and packing – see illustration*).

Section 3

STAR PERFORMERS IN THE WORLD OF CHURCHMANSHIP

In this section we celebrate the work of those individuals who have taken Churchmanship to new heights of ingenuity and effectiveness. Who better to learn from than these exceptionally talented star performers?

———JEREMY CROWN-CARSTAIRS——— THE ART OF AVOIDING CHORUSES WITH ACTIONS

There has been some very useful work done in the crucial area of how to avoid active participation in any activity occurring at the front of the church, including songs or choruses that involve embarrassing movements or gestures. In this connection, no one has taken the bull by the horns quite as dramatically as Jeremy Crown-Carstairs, a Churchman of many years' standing (and, as he himself dryly adds, doing nothing with his arms and feet if he has anything to do with it). Whenever, as happens fairly frequently, Crown-Carstairs moves to a new church, he makes a point of asking to be allowed to lead worship on the third or fourth Sunday that he is there, claiming that he knows 'a really great song that everyone can join in with'. We reproduce the words of his hideous song here, and they are freely available for use by any accredited Churchman. (*Available from Churchmanship Headquarters, price two pounds per copy including postage and packing – see illustration.*) A specific tune is not suggested, but Crown-Carstairs makes the valid point that there are quite a lot of all-purpose tunes floating around in the church ether. As their style falls somewhere between pantomime songs and worship choruses, it seems safe to assume that at least one is bound to adequately mould itself to the words.

We hunch our shoulders to our ears like galloping gnus
Then hop around the church like excited kangaroos
We make our tummies wibble-wobble just like jellies
We dive to the floor and we wriggle on our bellies
We leap up in the air like a jack-in-the-box
Then we turn to our neighbour and WE ALL SWOP SOCKS!

And are we getting weary? No!
Are we getting bored? No!
Are we feeling silly? No!
We do it for the Lord!

We do a Scottish hornpipe and we wiggle with our hips
We make a funny noise with our fingers and our lips
We croak like a frog (*Ribbit!*) growl like a bear (*Rrrrr!*)
We tap the ones in front of us and ruffle up their hair
We grab at both the shoulders of a mister or a miss
Then we all love each other with a GREAT BIG SLOPPY KISS!

And are we getting weary? No!
Are we getting bored? No!
Are we feeling silly? No!
We do it for the Lord!

We cuddle someone skinny and we dance with someone fat
We open up a Bible and we wear it like a hat
We climb up on our chairs and pretend we're chimpanzees
Then we roll our skirts and trousers up and feel each others' knees
And when the whole thing's over, with a chuckle and a grin
We tickle all the grumpy ones who've NOT BEEN JOINING IN!

And are we getting weary? No!
Are we getting bored? No!
Are we feeling silly? No!
We do it for the Lord!

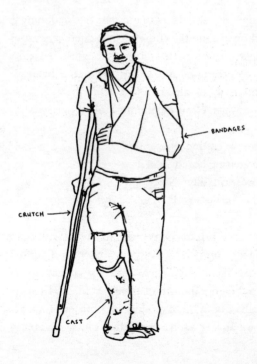

Once, for purposes of research, I attended one of these services at North Worthing Baptist church (*fully protected, of course, by the Churchman-approved Crutch, Cast and Bandaging set – available for hire from Headquarters at a cost of seven pounds per day – see illustration*). I was frankly amazed by the effect of this song, performed with enormous gusto and athleticism by Crown-Carstairs, who in his normal state is well known to be barely sentient and physically moribund. When the song had ended it was as though some terrible natural disaster had occurred in the church. A small number of glassy-eyed, grinning individuals had performed, or tried to perform, all the actions involved, but most folk were clinging to each other like survivors from the Titanic, white-faced and trembling as they struggled to recover from the shock of other people trying to take their socks off, feel their knees, give them a sloppy kiss or tickle them because they had failed to join in.

One young man, tall and gangly and dressed in a suit that was too short at the wrists and ankles, ducked out of the back door and sprinted through the car park and away into the distance rather in the style of Forrest Gump. Subsequently, I understand, he became a Presbyterian.

As far as Crown-Carstairs was concerned the whole thing was an enormous success. Obviously he was never asked to lead any singing ever again, and he was able to remain flopped down in his seat on all future occasions when others were leading choruses that called for people to join in with actions. No one dared to take the risk of unleashing the beast within Crown-Carstairs for a second time. Extreme measures, but Churchmanship at its best.

JULIUS BUTTERFIELD
THE ART OF EXPERTMANSHIP

Never one to withhold his modestly-framed opinions or pastoral advice from anyone who was too naïve to see through him or too sick or disabled to get away before he got into his stride, Julius Butterfield, a sadly-departed hero of our order, would sometimes be asked if he was a formally trained or ordained minister of some sort. His reply was a triumph of dual communication.

'What!' he would ejaculate with a little bewildered shake of the head, his face registering mild shock at the very idea that he might have considered something so alien and bizarre. 'Good heavens, no.'

How is it possible to convey humility and derision at exactly the same moment in a simple three-word phrase? Butterfield managed it admirably. Certainly his tone seemed to imply that someone as unimportant and ordinary as he could never seriously expect to rise to such heights of responsibility and authority. However, there was also a subtle but unmistakeable suggestion that boring old formal training would have had the effect of stifling the spontaneity and rich expressiveness of Butterfield's valuable ministry to others. Better, he appeared to be saying, to remain a humble but gifted amateur and be of some real use to people.

We can and should learn a lot from Butterfield. His adept and pioneering use of facial expression and the spoken word in parallel is a lesson and an inspiration to us all. I well recall, for instance, a morning in a church hall in Staines, when he was asked a factual question relating to a specific aspect of church history. Butterfield's ignorance in this and just about every other expert area of knowledge was, of course, profound, but dedicated students of Churchmanship will never allow themselves to be deflected or discouraged by such minor considerations. Butterfield handled it with great skill.

'Do you know,' he said wonderingly, placing his lower lip between his teeth and gazing up at the top left-hand corner of the hall with a wry smile of amused absorption on his face, 'I fancy there's more than one answer to that question.'

The impression given was that Butterfield had access to such a vast array of possible answers that he simply could not decide which one to select. Eventually he turned to a very mild, neatly sitting, terrified looking little man named Albert Bidden whose knowledge of church history was known to be encyclopaedic, and said, 'Bert, where are we on this? Would you go with the obvious?'

Albert Bidden, who to my certain knowledge has never been addressed or known as 'Bert' in his life, did cooperatively, if stutteringly, go for the obvious and probably only possible answer to the question that had been asked. But there was no doubt that Butterfield had scored heavily. In the eyes of all those present he and Albert Bidden were revealed as brothers and equals in scholarship, two men who knew such an immense amount about everything that they had to help each other out when it came to the distillation of all that knowledge into one simple, accessible fact.

———— DURHAM STEADMAN (1) ————
THE ART OF EXCUSEMANSHIP

One of our most talented members in past years has been Durham Steadman (*see following section on Special Relationshipmanship as well as the fine section above on Effective Communicationmanship*). He has brought a quality of drama and creativity to Churchmanship that makes his ploys a pleasure to witness or hear about. There was an occasion, for instance, when he was attending a small church that nestled in a fold of The Downs near Alfriston in Sussex. Steadman unexpectedly encountered William Burrows, the minister of the church, on a Monday morning in the quaint old village store. He reports that the conversation recorded here took place as both men were waiting to be served with the last slice of a famously delicious cold steak pie that was available from the delicatessen counter at the far end of the shop.

> MINISTER: Good to see you, Durham. (*mildly, after a pause*) Missed you in church yesterday morning – everything okay?
> STEADMAN: (*looking the minister straight in the eye and speaking in a tone embodying sorrow, pain and a certain splendid courage*) Yes, William, everything is absolutely okay, and I would like to caringly suggest that you missed me in church yesterday morning because your eyes and your heart were imprisoned by the solid, inflexible bars of impoverished expectation.

MINISTER: The solid, inflexible bars of . . . ?

STEADMAN: (*gazing into the distance in visionary style*) Yesterday morning, William, I worshipped in a cathedral more magnificent than any built by the soiled hands of man, where the roof above my head was a vast, shining bowl of sparkling azure blue, and the carpet beneath my feet was a soft, eternal expanse of emerald green.

MINISTER: You mean . . . ?

STEADMAN: (*well away now*) Where the choir consisted of the most natural musicians in creation, bursting with admiration and worship for he who sculpted the rolling landscape and commanded the purple-misted horizon to gently kiss the sky.

MINISTER: You mean you were up on the . . . ?

STEADMAN: And it was there, William, there where a man can cry aloud for the darkness that inhabits his soul, where he can cast down his wretched sins like slurry on the fertile, groaning land, where he can laugh for the very joy of redemption and pour out his supplications for a world that is torn and trembling with the agony of separation from God – it was there, I say, that I felt myself filled with the numinous essence. It was as though God had entered the sun itself and shards of light from that shining heart of love had descended to pierce and enter my heart. Yesterday morning, William, I was in church. Here is my question. Were you?

MINISTER: (*scratching his head*) Well, I thought I was . . .

At this point conversation between the two men was interrupted by a patter of spontaneous applause from other customers in the shop who had stopped what they were doing to listen. Steadman, who took the opportunity to swiftly buy the last piece of steak pie, had done his work well. Somehow he had managed to make Rattlington Methodist Church sound like some dismal little faithless hovel when compared with the 'Cathedral of the Skies'.

As a matter of history, Steadman had got up too late for church on that Sunday morning after forgetting to set his alarm. He'd driven up to Butt's Brow and taken a short, lazy stroll across to The

Eight Bells at Jevington, where he met a couple of mates for a long, indulgent lunch and a few pints, before being driven home slumped in the back of a taxi.

It was always pints. Durham Steadman never did anything by halves.

DURHAM STEADMAN (2)
THE ART OF SPECIAL RELATIONSHIPMANSHIP

The history of Churchmanship has been punctuated, as it were, by the emergence of those who are acknowledged experts in their own field. As we have seen in the previous section on Excusemanship, Durham Steadman (now retired) was just such a one. However, his exquisitely subtle ploys in the field of Special Relationshipmanship are equally memorable, if not more so.

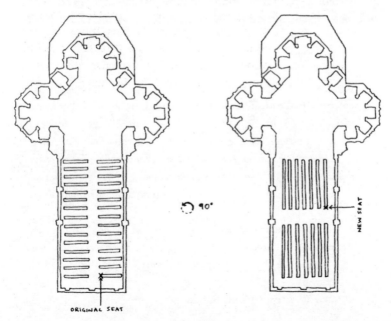

ORIGINAL SEAT

90°

NEW SEAT

I was once privileged to be present at a church meeting in Caterham that involved Steadman. It was called to resolve (among other things) the important question of whether the congregation should be turned ninety degrees so that they would face the side of the church instead of the end. I knew that Steadman was against change of this kind as it would automatically bring his place on the back row much nearer to the front, thus exposing him to all manner of unwelcome possibilities (*see diagram*).

As was his way, Durham Steadman sat looking serious and slightly worried as, one by one, people expressed their views. Eventually it became clear that his failure to contribute to the discussion was creating a sense of troubled insecurity in the others. Why had Steadman not spoken? Why was Steadman looking so grim? What would Steadman say when he did get going? Steadman, Steadman, Steadman. Every unspoken question seemed to ring with the name of Steadman.

Eventually, the discussion dribbled away into silence. All eyes finally came to rest on Steadman, but he just shook his head wearily and continued to say nothing. At last the chairman must have decided the time had come to sum up and, as far as I can recall, this was the ensuing dialogue.

CHAIRMAN: Well, I think we've probably gone about as far as we can go with the business of turning the church round. The general view here and in the wider church community seems to be that we might as well try it for a while and see how it works. After all . . . (*pauses as Steadman emits a faint but clearly audible sighing groan of depression and bewilderment, then continues uneasily*) Mr Steadman, you er, you've not expressed a view. Do you go along with what's been said, or . . . ?

STEADMAN: (*glancing up with an abrupt jerk of the head, as if surprised that he should be consulted, before replying quietly and rather darkly*) Sorry! Oh, well, no, it has nothing to do with what I think. My view is irrelevant.

CHAIRMAN: I see, well in that case –

STEADMAN: (*apparently gathering himself together with an effort and suddenly sounding quite snippy but very grown-up*) Okay. I will say something. I've listened very carefully to all the points that have been made. You talk about the wider community wanting this change to take place. Well, I only really have one thing to say. And, frankly, in the nicest possible way, you can take it or you can leave it. That so-called 'general view' that you talk about is not, I repeat, not what I'm hearing from *all the people who come to see me.*[9]

Steadman's genius has never been more clearly evidenced than in his use of the eight words at the end of this speech.

'. . . *all the people who come to see me*'.

Consider the subtle implications of this deceptively simple phrase. Who were *all* these people? Members of the church presumably, as their view was central to the discussion that had just taken place. But why should they *come to see* Steadman? Within those three-words does one detect the subtle but unmistakable suggestion of informal appointments made and kept, counselling required and given, provision of a refuge for trudging queues of unhappy folk who are unable to find understanding and sympathy through normal church channels, the establishment of a warm and caring environment where Steadman offers church in the true sense, church as they have always yearned for it to be, church as it was always meant to be? Church that is a glowing refuge in the midst of misguided, unsympathetic, near-atheistic darkness?

Did people really 'come to see' Steadman? How many came to see him? None? Twenty? Hundreds? Steadman seemed to imply a steady stream. How could anybody ever prove it to be otherwise? They could not. Steadman won the day. The congregation continued to face in the same direction as they had for thirty years, and Steadman went back to dozing quietly in his quick-exit position near the door.

---

[9]   My italics.

EDWARD FELLINGHAM — THE ART OF LOVABLE RUSTIC GRUMPMANSHIP

Many will recall the late Edward Fellingham, a lifelong church attendee in Durham and in recent years an admirably sharp but subtle thorn in the flesh of the New Light church in that distractingly beautiful city. Edward, who had been educated at Harrow but elected to use a gruff countryman's accent in the context of his Churchmanship activities, did a very skilful and strategically endearing line in Lovable Rustic Grumpmanship. When faith and works were being discussed, for instance, he would allow himself to be heard trenchantly muttering, 'I dunno 'bout faith and werrks an' awl that – I know faith werrks, an' that's always done me.'

In the end Edward became revered as some kind of primitive spiritual philosopher and was often asked for his practical, close-to-the-soil views on important issues arising in the church. Questions and answers arising from his Lovable Rustic Grumpmanship ploy include these three examples:

Q: What do you think about sex before marriage?
A: Well, you don't go a puttin' things where they didn't oughter be 'an you'll 'ave a tidy life.

Q: Do you ever doubt?
A: When I'm busy a-shearin' of sheep an' muckin' out the stalls (*stalls? for sheep?*) I sometimes think as 'ow I might do a bit o' doubtin' later on, but by the time I get inside 'an 'ave a bit o' dinner God an' me we'm (*we'm?*) both too tired to argue about it, so I just says thanks fer a good day, maister, and gets orf ter bed. Doubtin' an' all that – I guess its fer them as 'as too much time on their 'ands.

Q: Who will go to heaven?

A: God never tries ter tell me which of my animals to keep an'
   which ter send ter slaughter, an' I pay 'im the same compliment.
   Werrks well enough fer me. I look after my business an' 'e looks
   after 'is.

Edward, who had definitely never sheared any living thing other
than his own chin, nor mucked out so much as a gerbil in his entire
life, actually made his living buying and selling shares on the internet.
He was married to a stunningly beautiful Mexican senorita called Ines,
who spent her life catering for her husband's every whim in their seven-
bedroomed house in the Lanchester Valley west of Durham.

For his Sunday trips into the city Edward dressed in a crumpled
tweed suit with two buttons missing, a tight, sleeveless, threadbare
pullover that ended just above his wide leather trouser belt and heavy
black boots that looked as if they had survived the Second World
War. There were always bits of straw about. He drove a battered
old Lada to church and would meet any comments on the vehicle by
patting it on the roof as though it was a horse, and saying, 'Well, the
old gerrl suits me. She'll prob'ly larst fer years.' A fair assumption in
light of the fact that for six and a half days out of seven Edward was
driven around in an electric blue Bentley by his wife's father, Juan
Carlos Perrera Domingues.

——EDMUND CLAY - THE AMAZING—— REVERSING FEATURE PLOY

Edmund Clay's ability to plan and execute long-term ploys was
quite exceptional, and some of the results he achieved were truly
memorable.

The example we have chosen is quite extraordinary. Over a
long period of time, Clay consistently and unswervingly presented

a specific quirk or habit in his way of speaking whenever he was in listening range of a man called Barry Phelps. Phelps was one of those fleshy, shiny-eyed men who wear flowery shirts and see themselves as having a ministry in correcting the faults of others. It was Clay's extraordinarily ambitious intention to draw the other man into commenting on his verbal habit, and then to transfer that same habit to Phelps. Could it be done? A section of dialogue, secretly recorded by Edmund Clay wearing a wire in the Minehead Team Lounge at Spring Harvest 1997, allows us to answer that question.

PHELPS: Edmund, old mate, can I ask you something – in love?

CLAY: (*enthusiastically*) Sure, Barry. Fine. Right. Of course.

PHELPS: Well, I don't quite know how to put this . . .

CLAY: Just go ahead. Name it. Spit it out. Say what you mean.

PHELPS: Okay, well, you know you introduced the missionary film yesterday morning over in the alternative celebration? Remember that?

CLAY: You came? You were there? In the congregation? Did you get to that?

PHELPS: Yes, I did.

CLAY: Good! Great! Fantastic! Terrific!

PHELPS: So, anyway, I was watching you while you introduced the film and –

CLAY: Wonderful piece of film, wasn't it? Fantastic stuff to watch. Great to have those images up there. Terrific visual display.

PHELPS: Ah! Now, that's my point really.

CLAY: Something wrong with the film? You didn't like the pictures? Visuals not good enough? Not keen on the presentation?

PHELPS: No, no, the film was fine, Edmund. It was you. You've – well, you probably don't realize it, but you've started to say everything at least four times.

CLAY: (*apparently stunned by this information – despite having deliberately done this for months whenever he encountered Phelps*) Have I? Four times? Everything I say? Is that what I do? Do I really do that? I don't do that, do I?

PHELPS: Yes, I'm afraid you do.

CLAY: You could have fooled me. I didn't know. I had no idea. News to me.

PHELPS: Well, never mind, I'm sure now that I've shown you the problem you could easily change it. I think it must be like a bad habit you get yourself into. Maybe you catch it like a spiritual disease. Practise not saying things so many times and you'll be fine.

CLAY: (*brightening*) Yes, I could practise, couldn't I? I could work on improving it. I could make a real effort. I could – hah! There I go again.

PHELPS: You see! Only three and a half times. You'll soon sort it out.

CLAY: Right, so how long do you think it'll take? What sort of timescale are we looking at here? What's your estimate for – hah! I'll have to work at this.

PHELPS: A week. Seven days.

CLAY: Good. Excellent. (*Opens, then closes, his mouth. They laugh meaningfully together.*) So you think I'll be okay?

PHELPS: Well, I mean, you always were a fast learner. You do pick things up quickly. You don't have a problem with new ideas, do you?

CLAY: No, I don't. (*amazed pause*) Hey, this is amazing! I think it's gone already. What a clever chap you are.

PHELPS: Well done! Good for you. What an achievement. Congratulations!

CLAY: Thanks ever so much for your help.

PHELPS: Oh, it was nothing. No problem. Don't worry about it. You're welcome. Forget about it. Don't mention it.

CLAY: Barry, you don't really think it's a disease, do you, something you catch?

PHELPS: No, I was only joking. I wasn't serious. I didn't mean it. Negative to that. Absolutely not. Not at all. No way. That is not the case. No chance. Never in a million years. Of course not.

CLAY: Can I say something to you?

PHELPS: Sure. Fine. Right. Of course. Go ahead. Fire away.

CLAY: Well, I was just thinking – thank goodness you noticed!

PHELPS: *(slightly bewildered)* True. Yes. Spot on. Right. Er, absolutely . . .

Edmund Clay is one with his surname now, but his memory lives on in the hearts of all who appreciate extreme Churchmanship.

JASPER HEPWORTH
THE ART OF HIGH MORAL
GROUNDMANSHIP

As far as Churchmanship is concerned, Jasper Hepworth is without doubt one of the great innovators of our time. Not for Hepworth the quick trick, or the thinly veiled distraction. Hepworth is about long-term work and depth and completion, and a detailed account of his dealings with Michael Chapman illustrates this clearly.

Chapman was one of those slightly overweight, intelligent men working in local government who have nearly married once and never had the nerve to try again. A genuinely devout man who referred to his casual trousers as *slacks,* Chapman was troubled and handicapped by an almost total inability to express either very positive *or* very negative feelings. He became Hepworth's house group leader in the mid-eighties, a week or two after Hepworth began to attend the Fletcham Community Church near Westborne.

Hepworth's habitual ploy with house group leaders is easily expressed, but quite complex and demanding in execution. Put simply, it involves the cultivation of a close and even intimate relationship in situations outside formal church activities, while at the same time making life hell for the house group leader whenever the group meets. Chapman, being single and loaded above the Plimsoll line, as it were, with unexpressed frustrations, was ideally suited to Hepworth's approach.

At the end of the first house group Hepworth approached Chapman with an air of nervous humility. He explained that he was a stranger in a new town, and a single man just like Chapman. Would it be possible, he asked, for the two men to meet once a fortnight or so, just to have a drink and a chat together until Hepworth got to know a few other people in the church?

Michael Chapman, always genuinely keen to displace his troubles with practical assistance to others, agreed immediately. The two men got together once and sometimes twice a fortnight, either at the King's Head in North Street, or in Hepworth's bachelor flat opposite the Atrium Tearooms near the seafront.

Of course, within a very short time, Hepworth, who, as a trained Churchman, knew and knows the value of listening (*see Churchmanship pamphlet on Gathering Ammunition, two pounds including postage and packing – see illustration*), was able to relax and draw out his companion to such an extent that Chapman really did begin to feel that he had found a friend.

At the same time, Hepworth embarked on a careful campaign of disruption in the house group itself, using a mixture of cynicism and flippancy to kill moments of serious reflection or quiet prayer.

There was one autumn evening, for instance, when Michael Chapman said that each person there had to honestly consider if they had anything against anyone else in the group. If they did, they were to write it on a sheet of paper without anyone seeing. They would then go out onto the patio at the back and, in an act of symbolic release, burn the pieces of paper in a brazier that Chapman had lit ready for the purpose earlier in the evening.

'Don't hold anything back,' said Chapman seriously. 'Whatever and however much you feel, make sure you write it down and then let it just burn away.'

Ten minutes later the group processed in a solemn, silent queue out of the French windows and around the flaming brazier, dropping their scrunched-up pieces of paper into the blaze as they went. The atmosphere was one of meaningful concentration – until, that is, Hepworth reached the brazier and pulled out a very large, scribbled-on toilet roll which he held flamboyantly above his head before dropping it with a 'whump!' into the depths.

'Sorry, folks,' he said, cackling like a hyena. 'Michael said we had to get it all down, so I did! I hate you all! Bless you – only kidding!'

Most people laughed, the exercise was ruined and Chapman fumed like a ventless boiler. It was Hepworth himself who had very seriously and encouragingly put forward the brazier idea when the two men met at the pub earlier in the week. Now he had sabotaged it. Why?

For the next eighteen months the pressure continued to build inside Michael Chapman. As a general rule Hepworth was flippantly negative, dismissive and argumentative when serious biblical or teaching points were being made, and withdrawn and impenetrably sulky when the group was supposed to be relaxing and having fun. Meanwhile the two men continued to meet socially and relate in a completely different way. It began to drive Chapman mad. The combination of his own repressive personality and the confusing nature of his dual relationship with Hepworth meant that any efforts he might have made to express his feelings were strangled at birth.

At last he went to the other elders of the church and announced that he was resigning as a house group leader and as an elder, and that he would be leaving the church altogether in a few weeks' time.

They asked why. Chapman went puce and nearly burst but was unable to produce any words other than a confused, muttered reference to Jasper Hepworth. That was all he would say.

Invited to an elders' meeting the next week, Hepworth expressed hurt amazement on hearing that he had been mentioned by Chapman in connection with his resignation.

'I'm genuinely puzzled,' he said in a limp, lost sort of way. 'Just between the six of us here, I've spent hours with Mike listening to his problems and trying to be, you know, a friend in need. I don't understand it. I feel a bit – well, never mind how I feel, Mike's the one that matters – what do you think I ought to do?'

This was exactly the right question for Hepworth to ask. All Churchmen have been carefully taught to be aware that elders tend to be insecure about their authority. Correct strategy is to always ask them for guidance and advice. This can be productive in terms of finance and license. In this case they suggested, as Hepworth had known they would, that he should pray about it and then act on the leading he received. The next day he phoned one of the elders and said that after an uneasy night of prayer and consideration (he had actually had a long, lingering bath and then, assisted by three large brandies, had slept like a baby all night) he had decided to go and see Chapman in order to 'put things right'. But, he added, he wondered if it would be better for one of the elders to come along as well – for Mike's sake.

Thus, the scene was set for Hepworth to demonstrate the art of High Moral Groundmanship at its height. The most important part of the conversation at Michael Chapman's house was entirely predictable, certainly as far as Hepworth was concerned.

> HEPWORTH: (*sitting on the edge of the sofa, leaning forward, arms dangling in front of him, exuding humility and good intentions*) Mike, mate, we're here because – well, because I gather your decision to step down and leave the church and all that has got something to do with me. (*holding his hands out, palms upward, as he continues*) I have to say, Mike, that I'm a bit . . . (*sighing heavily*) What am I? Okay, yes, I'm

a bit upset, and pretty confused as well. I just don't understand what it is that I've done, and I want to clear it up. Obviously I must have hurt you somehow without realizing it, and if that is the case I'd rather know. And I apologize unreservedly for anything I might have done without realizing it. So – this is a chance to get the air cleared and start all over again. Are you with me so far?

CHAPMAN: (*so painfully packed with unsaid things that he is incapable of producing anything coherent*) Prsgm!

HEPWORTH: (*leaning back and spreading his arms and legs wide as if opening his whole being up to attack*) So let me have it, Mike. Whatever it is now is the time to get it off your chest. I want you to tell me every single thing you've got against me and give me a chance to say sorry and – you know – hopefully get things back on track again. Not just with me, of course, but with the church as well. We don't want to lose you, Mike. (*directing a shy little hopeful smile at the accompanying elder as if seeking confirmation*) That's right isn't it, Steve?

STEVE: (*nodding encouragingly*) That's absolutely right!

CHAPMAN: (*looking like a human being trapped inside a large boiled vegetable, and still unable to distil feelings into words*) Grprms!

I need hardly add that Michael Chapman never did succeed in expressing any of the bewildered resentment that he felt towards Hepworth. It was too complicated, too late, too alarming and too impossible for one such as Chapman to squeeze out the words that might have made a difference. He left the church and Hepworth won.

Hepworth himself, of course, exhibited mournful regret about the whole matter, and he received considerable sympathy over the need to, as he plaintively put it, 'find a way to rebuild his trust in relationships'.

'After all,' he would say, 'I gave Michael every chance to tell me exactly how I'd upset him, and there was nothing. What more could I do? The whole thing's such a puzzle. Still, there we are . . .'

And he would click his tongue and shake his head at the sadness and the mystery of it all and be comforted by others.

It may interest readers of this report to know that the tale of Jasper Hepworth and Michael Chapman provokes a fairly uniform response in Churchmanship students when I relate it to them.

'Is it not the case, Professor Caws,' they tend to ask me, 'that Hepworth is a cynical, manipulative predator, who has demonstrated an unscrupulous lust for power over another human being with no regard whatsoever for that person's happiness and well-being?'
My reply is always the same.

'All of those things may be true,' I tell them, 'but please do not feel threatened. He has many faults as well.'

Section 4

CHURCH OF ENGLANDMANSHIP

The discerning Churchman or woman will be acutely aware in these dangerously ecumenical days that it is foolish to assume one is truly safe in any denominational setting. The Church of England is a first-rate example of this unfortunate trend. Gone are the days when stalwarts of the Parish Church would casually enquire of their vicar in the church porch after the service, 'Do you ever come across any of those born-again people?' And the guardian of their souls would shake his head and smile one of those reassuringly well-educated, culturally-infused, cricket-loving smiles and assure the questioner that that sort of thing was a phase at best, and a wrong understanding at worst.

Nowadays Anglican churches range from dead to wildly charismatic and from socially aware to stubbornly and attractively unwilling to look outwards – not to mention all the gradations between these extremes.

The new millennium has seen an increasing number of ploys designed and developed for use by Churchmen and women in these unsettling days. Some are what one might term 'broad principles'. William Custer, who collects membership of Anglican churches as other people collect scarce stamps of obscure nations, reports consistent success with a simple ploy known as *Always Going a Little Farther the Other Way than Anybody Elsemanship*. It is, says Custer, virtually self-working. His words:

If you find yourself in a stiff little country parish where most people think that Baptism in the Spirit is something to do with preserving peaches, then make sure you become known as the one who is always gently pushing towards modernization and a greater understanding of spirituality and the work of the Holy Spirit. However, you must be very careful not to push too hard. Success would spoil everything.

If, on the other hand, you land in a church where the pews have gone; a proper sound system has been put in; liturgy might as well be a vegetable dish in the local Indian restaurant as far as anyone in the congregation is concerned; children don't leave and go to King's Church in the big ex-factory on the industrial estate as soon as they're allowed to; the vicar speaks *Esperanto* under his breath and takes parties off to New Wine; and the whole place is heading for a split, then you need to be the one who introduces friendly but firm reminders of the fact that 'tradition and history have their own very profound part to play in a church that truly wishes to be led by the Holy Spirit'.

You cannot go far wrong in this kind of church, continues Custer, as long as, to use his words: 'The Holy Spirit crops up somewhere in the stuff you're saying.'

COMMUNION PLOYS

Something about an Anglican communion service – possibly the tension-filled combination of mobility and solemnity – cries out for attention from the alert Churchman or woman.

Much has been said and written about the 'Exchanging of the Peace', but we at Churchmanship Headquarters can do no more than endorse the views and advanced techniques of David Trump of Cornwall (*see section on Weekend Awaymanship*). Trump writes:

For those joining a new congregation, procedure regarding the Exchanging of the Peace is perfectly straightforward. For the first few communion services that he attends the Churchman should ignore the nervous meandering and muttering that will invariably surround him. He should instead move confidently around the church, cordially greeting a selection of men and warmly embracing the oldest and plainest women he can find. Offer a gruffly polite, distracted and arms' length handshake to attractive women (*see illustration*), but only if there is time left over in the allocated period.

After consistently adhering to this behaviour for five or six communion services, the Churchman will be firmly established as one of those people (rare to the point of extinction, despite the brainless burblings of people taking part in audience participation television shows) who is attracted not by outward appearances, but by the *real* person inside. He may now approach one of the good-looking women with a quiet, adult, approving smile designed to communicate to her that, in his eyes, she has made the grade at last. She has something fine and good inside her, and so she qualifies for a hug from him – *despite* being young and attractive.

The Churchman should continue to strategically spread his attentions, but by this point the die will have been cast. People will know it is a privilege to be hugged by him during the Exchanging of the Peace. He may even find, as I have done from time to time, something of a queue forming.

During the communion itself a deceptively elementary but useful ploy can be carried out against those officials, usually church-wardens, who move slowly backwards down the centre aisle of the church, leaning down and indicating to the person sitting at the end of each row that it is time for them to stand and join the queue for communion. Close observation reveals that these individuals never quite speak. They gesture with one arm, and although their lips certainly move and twitch as though something is trying to come out, intelligible words are conspicuous by their absence.[10]

Proceed in the following way.

Having ensured that you are sitting on the sixth row from the front in the pew nearest to the centre aisle, wait until the church-warden does his leaning down, arm gesturing, lip-twitching thing and then say in friendly but distracted tones, 'I'm sorry, I didn't quite catch that.'

'People are about patterns.'[11] This is generally true of those who attend traditional churches, and it is specifically the case with those who perform regular tasks within the church. A species of temporary paralysis seems to set in when a familiar pattern is interrupted or broken. On the occasion when I last used this ploy the dialogue began and ended most satisfactorily.

---

[10] Jane Britton, who currently leads our half-yearly three-week course on *Clouding the Issue for New Converts*, tells me that she once achieved great success in this context by saying something completely unintelligible in a very low voice *to* the churchwarden. After five or six attempts to understand what she had said he began to hyperventilate and had to be stretched out horizontally on the floor of the vestry.

[11] Butterfield, 1986.

ME: I'm sorry, Don, I didn't quite catch that.

WARDEN: Mmfn! Grrdfm! Would you . . . ? Do you . . . ?

ME: I'm sorry, I don't hear very well on this side. Could you speak up just a little bit?

WARDEN: (*gesturing hopefully and mumbling incoherently*) It's your turn . . . Are you going to . . . ?

ME: Look, I'm really sorry, but I simply can't hear what you're saying.

WARDEN: (*raising his voice and making a huge effort to produce a whole sentence*) Did you want to go up for communion this morning?

ME: (*smiling and nodding and settling back comfortably*) Oh, I see. Well, yes, I will be going up for communion just as soon as it's my turn.

WARDEN: (*with a sort of contained apoplexy*) But it's your turn now!

ME: (*reproachfully*) Well, I wish someone had taken the trouble to tell me. I'm holding up all these other people in my row. We really ought to have someone letting us know when it's time to join the line. That used to be your job, didn't it, Don? Anyway, nice to chat, but we should be getting up to the front. Would you mind taking a step back so that I can get out into the aisle . . . ?

Butterfield at Communion

Julius Butterfield, something of an expert on Communion Ploys, would occasionally take communion and then duck round behind the backs of the other communicants and join the queue for a second time. Butterfield maintains that not a single minister in any of the churches he has attended ever questioned or commented on a member of his congregation turning up for 'seconds'. Even on the solitary occasion when he presented himself for a staggering *third* dispensation of bread and wine, the vicar in question simply stared for a moment like a man hypnotized, rocked backwards and forwards a little on his largish feet, and then continued as though nothing had happened.

Butterfield was also the originator of the now widely used Bread or Blessing? ploy. This technique is applicable in churches where the minister suggests that those who do not wish to take communion but would like a prayer of blessing should bring their hymnbook up to the rail and hold it in front of them instead of extending cupped hands to receive the bread. Butterfield's deceptively simple ploy is to hold the hymnbook in front of him with his right hand and extend his cupped left hand as if to receive the bread (*see illustration*). When the perplexed minister leans in close to ask if bread or blessing is required Butterfield remains completely motionless with his eyes closed, neither speaking nor moving until the celebrant has moved on. Over several years of executing this ploy Butterfield reports that, in such situations, he has had the blessing pressed upon him but no bread, the bread but no blessing, the bread and the blessing and, on a Sunday morning when the minister must have become more flustered than usual, a white silk handkerchief with the priest's initials monogrammed in blue thread on one corner.

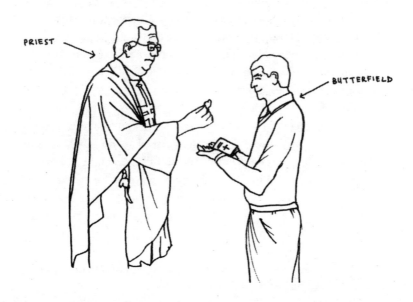

PRIEST

BUTTERFIELD

RESPONSEMANSHIP

Generally speaking, it is with sinking hearts that Anglicans receive an invitation to respond to prayers with a particular set of words that are not included in the prayer book. Some of these responses are simply too miserably dull and drab for words. Others, in churches where there is no overhead projector, are just half a sentence too long for congregations to easily remember what has to be said. In this latter context Churchwoman Carol Wiseman of Norwich, who attends an Anglican church near Magdalene Street in the old part of the city, has developed a ploy that is well worth replicating by other Gamesmen and women who are keen to remove this blight from their services. A piquant aspect of Carol's ploy is that it successfully disconcerts the *entire* congregation – a major accomplishment in our view.

Following is an extract from Carol's report.

'I have always found it an advantage in church life to maintain an image of demure mousiness (I save my hot pink lycra, giant shiny scrunchies and platform shoes for clubbing and raves), and to ensure that any speaking I do to the congregation is in a mumbling, tentative voice that is barely audible. The provision of a microphone is not a problem. Obviously on karaoke nights at The Gay Pelican I virtually swallow the damn thing, but in church I am at pains to demonstrate that fear and self-consciousness prevent me from properly using such a threatening item of technology. As you can imagine, this has been of enormous benefit. I am rarely asked to do anything that involves speaking from the front of the church. Recently, however, I have endured and had to deal with a new wave of encouragement to 'overcome my nerves'. Probably because of this our booming, amiable vicar, who is built and dressed like a large ceramic salt cellar, was more than happy to let me lead the prayers when I tremulously asked if I might be allowed to have a go.

'Would it be all right if I invited the congregation to do a special response?' I enquired timidly.

'Of course, dear lady,' he replied, doing a little silent clap with his hands, 'that would be delightful. We should all *so* enjoy and value that. And will you be requiring the overhead projector?'

'Oh, my goodness, no,' I fluttered. 'I really don't understand that sort of thing. Besides, it will all be very simple.'

Two Sundays later, as the third hymn came to an end, I walked up to the lectern and addressed the congregation in my usual uncertain way.

'I am going to say – well, I'm going to *try* to say some prayers, and perhaps you wouldn't mind – you don't have to, of course, but it would be lovely if you would – just say a special response at the end of each one.'

Encouraging nods and smiles from quite a lot of people, all willing me to do well.

'Thank you very much. So, when I say:

' *"Grant this prayer."*

'I'd like you to say:

' *"Thus we assert that which was not believed by those who proclaimed it to us in former days but is now confirmed by those who have sealed it with their prayerful assent."* '

Ignoring the wave of panic that immediately flittered through the church, I went on to say seven prayers in all, each accompanied by 'Grant this prayer . . . etc.' Most people did have a go at getting the response right, but in the end they didn't sound at all like an Anglican congregation. They sounded like a hundred and fifty depressed drunks trying to remember their addresses to give to a policeman on a Friday night. It was Babel without the tower.

Having apologized profusely and slightly tearfully at the end of the service, I was made much of during coffee time. The vicar gently suggested that public prayer might not be my absolute forte, and that I should explore alternative giftings as the Lord revealed them to me. I agreed sadly.

Result!

Section 5
WEEKEND AWAYMANSHIP

Here at Churchmanship Headquarters we are always open to the introduction of new ideas, and so it is with considerable pleasure that we report a communication from David Trump of Bude in Cornwall. So successfully has Trump learned and internalized the principles of Churchmanship that, despite believing nothing about anything, he is beginning to be asked to speak at church weekends all over the west of England. Here is an extract from his recent letter.

As you will know, making a success of these weekends away will often involve the need to wrong-foot the minister of the church. If he or she is egotistical and overbearing it can be very difficult to maintain the air of deep, genial authority that is so necessary in this situation. It is, however, fairly easy to deal with. A little careful research usually does the trick. A recent Anglican church weekend was a good example. In the hustle and bustle of Friday evening arrivals, and (most helpfully) at a time when quite a lot of people were complaining bitterly about the inappropriateness of rooms allocated to them by the vicar's wife, I managed, through a combination of sympathetic questioning and solemn agreement with absolutely everything said to me, to discover that Reverend Coltbarm was opposed to just about every aspect of change, and particularly to the ordination of women. From then on it was all plain sailing. After a plummy but fulsome introduction from the vicar, I began my first session on the Saturday morning in a roistering, vigorous manner.

'Can I start by saying how very refreshing it is to find myself among folk who have escaped the straitjacket of the past and are willing to see and respond to the beckoning hand of God as it calls us into the future? Well done! In conversations with many of you yesterday evening I learned of your flexibility in matters of liturgy and worship and style of communion and the role of clergy and especially, if I may say so, your warm and open-hearted acceptance of women into the ministry. And this –'

I paused and turned to indicate the vicar before continuing.

'This must be a tribute to Reverend Coltbarm, who has led you unswervingly along the pathway of change like the great and humble man of God that he is. I believe a round of applause would not be inappropriate.'

As you know better than I do, Christian groups are wonderfully biddable. The resulting applause, delivered with contrasting elements of vindictiveness and puzzlement, was accompanied by a flash of white light as someone in the congregation took a photograph. I was fortunate enough to obtain a copy of this photograph and I enclose it for your interest. It clearly depicts the expression on the Reverend Coltbarm's face as he receives a round of applause from his congregation for doing and being the exact opposite of what he does and is. I will always treasure it. I wish I had been able to also record the spluttering noise (not unlike a death-rattle) that he made.

If, on the other hand, the minister or pastor involved is a truly humble, flexible individual, a completely different ploy is required. The procedure I would like to offer is a tried and tested solution to the problem. It is best used during the Friday night 'getting-to-know-you' session when the atmosphere is, in any case, fairly breathless and fraught, and quite a lot of people have suddenly realized they are going to miss a programme on the telly that they always watch and are already wishing they had not put their names down.

This is how I began my Friday night 'chat' to the Blakeham Community Church weekend at Hopwood House in February. Students of Churchmanship will be well aware of the need for vocal delivery to hover somewhere between levity and gravity, so that the desired effect can be achieved and the subsequent disclaimer justified.

'Good evening! My name is Nigel Trump and I'm your speaker for the weekend. I hope you're all settled in and comfortable and looking forward to the next couple of days. Now, while I was planning my talks for the weekend I gave your pastor a ring and just asked him to give me a rundown on the type of people who'd be coming along. Very helpfully he sent a list of all the names with a comment next to each one. So I thought I'd just read out a few of them – not the names, of course, that wouldn't be fair, just the comments. See if you recognize yourselves! Hopefully it'll help us get a picture of who's around this weekend. I've got the minister's list, so here we go. The first one's a woman:

> Every cell in her body is annoying, but we'd never hear the last of it if she didn't come.

> Claims to be a believer, but if he's a Christian I'm a Methodist.

> Very attractive young lady – got a bit of a thing for me, I think.

> Pillar of the church. A big thick thing that holds everything up and restricts vision.

> Off with the fairies. Will only be present with us in a very limited sense.

> Frankly obnoxious, but rolling in it, so worth hanging on to until the church repairs get sorted, if you get my drift.

> Just a huge mouth on legs. Graduate of the Schwarzenegger School of ministry. Needs a good slapping in my estimation.

> If this family were pews we'd have them ripped out and get something more useful and attractive to put in their place.

> A frightful frump to look at, but co-operative and useful in a lumbering, oxen-like way.

By the time I reached the end of my list a very satisfactory amalgam of laughter, consternation and downright anger was rolling around the hall. As every Churchman and woman knows, all groups of this kind, or indeed of any kind, are divided (metaphorically) into the cheap seats at the back and the expensive ones at the front. The collision of ribaldry and concern is always a fruitful one.

Of course, I immediately laughed and expressed amazement that anyone might have believed that the list was a serious one, but my aim was already achieved. Seeds of mistrust and unhelpful flippancy had been securely sown, and it would be a poor Churchman who was unable to bring such promising new life to glorious fruition.

————DOING MY BITMANSHIP————

Designed for those attending church weekends who are not in positions of leadership, this sub-ploy of Weekend Awaymanship incorporates the *Making the Best of It* strategy of Churchman Arnold Bloom, together with Durham Steadman's inspired and much celebrated *Rolling Your Sleeves Up and Getting on with It* labour-saving initiative.

In the previous section we hinted at the fact that church weekends away can frequently begin with widespread dissatisfaction and rancour as people find to their horror that they have been placed in rooms where they will be on their own, rooms where they will not be on their own, rooms that are too hot, rooms that are too cold, rooms facing the front, rooms facing the back, rooms facing the sides, rooms over the kitchen, rooms next to the kitchen, rooms under the kitchen, rooms behind the kitchen, rooms that do not have an en-suite bathroom, rooms that are too big and scary, rooms that are too small and claustrophobic, rooms where the pipes make horrible noises, rooms next to noisy children, rooms that are too quiet and rooms that, for a myriad reasons, are not worth the extortionate amount of money that has been paid for them. All this is quite apart from such matters as special diets inadequately catered for, insufficient clothes hangers, no telly, malfunctioning heaters, draughts, beds that are too hard, beds that are too soft and spiders in the sink.

Durham Steadman describes correct procedure for Doing My Bitmanship in this context:

> Success in this ploy depends on the Churchman positively bursting with energy and exuding goodwill for the first three hours of the weekend. He will be found everywhere – carrying cases, helping people find their way around the building, shifting tables and chairs, fetching and carrying during the evening meal with unshakeable good humour and, when dinner is finished, rolling his sleeves up with enormous gusto and calling out things like, 'Well, let's get to the jolly old washing up! The sooner we start the sooner it'll be finished. What do you say, boys and girls? Then we can all relax.'[12]
>
> And, once the washing up is finished, that is exactly what the Churchman will do. He will relax and almost certainly be waited on hand and foot by those who witnessed his initial explosion of charitable effort. In fact, he will do nothing at all for the rest of the weekend. Having printed on the minds of all those present an indelible picture of himself as a willing worker for the benefit of others he will not lift a finger to help anyone but himself from that moment until he leaves for home on Sunday afternoon.

At the Sunday service a week after the last weekend when I used this ploy I was publicly thanked for my untiring and indefatigable efforts on behalf of others throughout the church weekend.

---

[12] Anton Devrais of the Restoration Church of Christ near Wincanton suggests that the benefits of this ploy are even greater if the Churchman can ensure that he is sitting with a group of happily chatting men from the church when he sets off to begin his flurry of hard work. Correct procedure in this situation involves the Churchman standing up and interrupting the conversation by saying, 'You chaps carry on putting the world to rights – I fancy there's a bit of good old boring work to be done around the place. I've never been very good at pontificating, but I can still do my share on the practical side.' Sometimes it will be possible to almost *cut* the silence and the shame.

How to Lose the Children

A recent letter from Len Carnon of Indian Queens in Cornwall offers a suggestion that may be of great interest to the Churchman or woman who wishes to gain kudos during a church weekend away in return for doing absolutely nothing. Carnon writes:

> During our last weekend away at Barham House down on the Lizard in June, I offered to take all the ten- to thirteen-year-old kids off everyone's hands on the Saturday afternoon and 'do something with them'. Of course parents and elder brothers and sisters were more than keen on this idea. They were ecstatic, and pathetically grateful to me for filling up my spare time when I could have been relaxing like all the others.
>
> 'Don't you worry yourselves,' I said with a breezy cheeriness that I'd been working very hard on. 'I'd like to spend a few hours with the young folks. I like young'uns. Off with you and have a good time. We'll see you later.'
>
> Filling the church bus up with children, I drove five miles out into the country, then stopped at the side of the road to explain that I would be dropping them in pairs at random spots in the narrow lanes that criss-cross the peninsula.
>
> 'After that,' I said, 'I shall be driving around the lanes all afternoon trying to catch sight of you. Any I spot have to get in the bus and help me look for the others. Anyone who gets back to Barham without me seeing them gets a little prize.'
>
> That was that. Once I'd dropped them all off I found a nice little shop with a café and a garden, bought a paper and dozed in the sunshine all afternoon. Meanwhile the kids must have been ducking into ditches and hiding behind hedges every time they heard a vehicle coming. Before leaving I bought a bag of cheap sweets to give out to the 'winners', and that was that. A good time had by all! I think quite a lot of them even got back in time for the evening meal.

─────────── A WORD OF CAUTION ───────────

Hopefully, this report has made it implicitly clear to students and members alike that there is a line which cannot be crossed without producing a counterproductive result as far as Churchmen and women are concerned. Julius Butterfield confesses that, as a young man, he made just such a mistake in the course of a late summer weekend away with the congregation of Wareham-East Methodist church at a school in Kimmeridge on the coast of Dorset.

After supper on the Saturday evening the young Churchman offered to lead a midnight walk that would start up the hill in a northerly direction, then circle round west and south and eventually arrive back at the school. There were quite a number of takers. Everyone said it sounded like a lot of fun. Accordingly, at about eleven-thirty that night, Butterfield, who had grown up in the area and knew it extremely well, led his cheery group, well armed with torches, along winding lanes and footpaths for about an hour until they arrived in a grassy space at the side of a large field.

'How about we stop here for a few minutes, friends,' he suggested brightly, 'and have a little time of praise and worship?'

Song sheets were given out and soon the warm night air was filled with the sound of joyous songs and hymns.

Butterfield was the only one present who knew that a farmhouse stood immediately behind the thin hedge that bordered the field. He was also the only one who knew that the farmer who lived there would be enjoying, or trying to enjoy, a deep and refreshing sleep after working frantically hard for the whole of the past fortnight to get his crops in.

Butterfield managed to slip away unnoticed into the darkness as the third ringing repetition of 'Majesty' neared its end, but the outpouring of the songsters continued unabated. They really were in fine voice, that little choir.

The farmer may have been a very patient man under normal circumstances, but it is perhaps understandable that, as the choir eventually embarked on a triumphantly lively rendition of 'Bringing in the Sheaves', something must have snapped in him.[13] There was a sound between a scream and a muffled, guttural oath, followed by a heavy sash-window being flung open and a series of loud explosions as the farmer, half-crazed from lack of sleep, fired his shotgun into the sky above the source of his torture.

The terrified choir broke ranks and fled into the night. One or two failed to find their weary way back to the school until three in the morning.

The art of Churchmanship is ideally a subtle one. Butterfield himself would certainly agree, in the light of age and experience, that we should not be responsible for organizing something reminiscent of a Tarentino film. Our object is to disconcert people, not to have them massacred.

---

[13]   The last straw?

Section 6

THE ART OF STEPMANSHIP

Those of us who take responsibility for the development of Church-manship have always tried to make it clear that students are not bound by rules and regulations. We would prefer to say that they are directed into favourable positions by the application of firm guidelines. Aspects of Stepmanship offer a helpful illustration of this principle.

In this area the guidelines could not be clearer. A true Churchman will never resign from any church post or responsibility because he is 'fed up with helping people' or 'doesn't want to be bothered with it any more' or 'can't see any real pay-off in the situation' or is 'sick to the back teeth of people clucking around him like retarded hens'. Or indeed for any other similarly good and genuine reason. Instead, he will announce his intention to *step back*, *step down* or *step apart*.

Publicly announced decisions made by Churchmen or women for their own benefit (virtually a tautology) should always be perceived by the rest of the community as reluctant but necessary acts of sacrificial love, and this is what Stepmanship helps to achieve in the area of resignations and the abandonment of tiresome responsibilities.

A brief analysis of the three varieties of Stepping might be helpful at this point, and I am indebted to David Withers of Hinton-in-the-hedges for his valuable contribution to this section. David remains a closet Churchman, but he has done some very sound and productive work for us in his own unobtrusive way.

———————— (1) STEPPING BACK ————————

One of my own particular favourites, this phrase carries with it connotations of quiet, measured wisdom. It suggests that, although relinquishing his responsibilities, the Churchman is maintaining a watching brief, prepared at any moment to assist or support the one chosen to take his place. Many years ago, in the seventies, I used a special turn of phrase (borrowed from an old Churchmanship manual) when addressing the elders at a Brethren church near Dunstable where, in a weak moment, I had accepted responsibility for organizing a cleaning rota for the church conveniences.

'The Lord would have me step back from the toilets for a season.'

I had little idea of what a season might be in this context, other than one of the four divisions of the year (I suppose, on that basis, the summer of that particular year might have been the season when one would be best advised to step back from and generally avoid public toilets), and the construction of the sentence struck me as impenetrably odd, but the response certainly fulfilled my expectations. After being gravely thanked for my services to the church in the past and my obedience to this present call, I was able to step back from the toilets forever. Just as well. It was a nasty, grotty little job, which too often ended up with me doing it myself because volunteers rang in with 'problems at home' or simply didn't turn up.

———————— (2) STEPPING DOWN ————————

Dripping with humility even as honeycombs drip with sweetness, this wonderfully emotive term can, if used properly, paint a rather beautiful picture of the weary saint – a warm, sad smile of self-abnegation on his patient, lined features, bowing beneath the weight of an awareness that he must decrease in order that some other dear soul may increase. A general perception that the Churchman is generously giving up space for another person's benefit has to be a very attractive bonus. Not only does he get out of whatever miserably tedious job he has made the mistake of volunteering for, but he also carries an aura of spiritual heroism into the future. Valuable currency indeed for the keen Churchman.

(3) STEPPING APART

Here is an interesting variety of Stepmanship. The implication here is that the person concerned has been temporarily called onto a different and probably higher plane of spiritual awareness in order to receive, as it were, orders for the future. Daniel Feltham, a usefully ethereal-looking individual and a notoriously hard drinker and atheist who trained with me years ago at Churchmanship Headquarters, claims that he became venerated as an almost Padre Pio-like figure after 'stepping apart' from his role as chairman of the church hall committee in order to 'await a word from the Lord that is to come'.

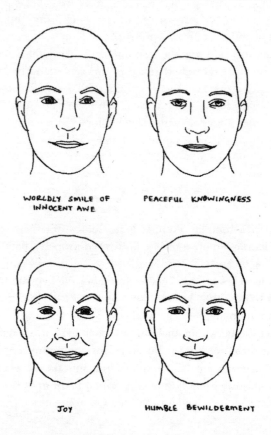

WORLDLY SMILE OF
INNOCENT AWE

PEACEFUL KNOWINGNESS

JOY

HUMBLE BEWILDERMENT

In the weeks and months following his resignation, Daniel (who, to his credit, takes his work as a Churchman extremely seriously) would, with quietly subtle ostentation, drift away from church groups without offering any explanation and allow himself to be discovered later – leaning bonelessly against a wall staring yearningly into the distance or sitting with his legs stuck out straight like a child on a flower-strewn bank, an other-worldly smile of innocent awe and joy (*courses available in the cultivation of this and other useful expressions on application, prices vary – see illustration*) on his face.

Later, as his mystical reputation reached its height, Daniel would hurriedly hide the palms of his hands with troubled self-consciousness when anyone approached, but I and the majority of my colleagues here at Headquarters feel that this was going just a little too far – even for a Churchman.

——SPENDING MORE TIME WITH—— THE FAMILYSHIP

One additional comment on the subject of Stepmanship. Byron Marnott, an old friend from Sussex and one of that surprisingly large group that one might call 'unconscious' Churchmen, frequently employed his own version of Stepmanship. Byron was a man who plunged headlong into church activities, participating with huge enthusiasm until he reached the point where steady hard work was required. He would then widely publish the fact that he was going through a period of 'painful inner debate'. This always culminated in a decision to resign because his family was suffering as a result of his involvement in church activities.

There is no doubt that Byron's technique was excellent, and his public statements on these occasions could have come straight from the pages of the Churchmanship manual. I can see him now, standing up straight and brave and true at the front of the church as he spoke:

Friends, I have recently been forced to ask myself what the Lord will hold me accountable for when I finally meet him face to face. My family has been given to me as a sacred trust, and I think, for the time being at least, they must become my priority. I hope therefore that you will understand the necessity for me to stand down from the work that I have been doing in helping to maintain the fabric of our building – a work, I might add, that I love.

Masterly stuff, and the little emotional catch in his voice as he lowered his head and delivered that final ludicrous phrase (Byron's wife reports that he became red-faced and vituperatively abusive whenever he was called on to perform the smallest task) was especially impressive. The mistake that Byron made (and this is always a possible pitfall for those who are not properly trained by us in strategic restraint) was that he repeated his effects without any variation at all. There is only so much plunging and painful inner debating and quitting that one person can do before even a URC congregation gets wise to what is going on. When challenged as to his motivation, Byron, who has never been able to see or acknowledge 'The Churchman Within', was deeply shocked.

STEPPING UP?

As an addendum to this section it is interesting to note that we have been asked by a number of students if, in our view, there can ever be a good reason for Stepping Up. The official reply is a qualified affirmative. There are certain circumstances in which this is the very best thing that a Churchman or woman can do, but great care must be taken if disaster is to be avoided. Once again, timing is everything.

Let us imagine that a really arduous role has opened up in the church – one that will require time and energy beyond normal expectations. Herein lies a perfect opportunity for the willing Churchman or woman. Wait until you are *absolutely sure* that the task has been taken up by someone else, and then, as soon as you possibly can, *Step Up* with vibrant enthusiasm to volunteer yourself for the role. All the potential for a perfect result is there – all of the kudos (and considerable sympathy) with none of the hard work or responsibility.

A note of warning, however. The appropriate level of visible disappointment to be demonstrated in this context is a matter for the individual to assess, *but care must be taken*. Dawn Cole, one of our northern members, gave the impression of being so inconsolably grief-stricken on hearing her application was too late, that the woman who had just undertaken the job was asked by the chief elder to take pity on her and resign so that Dawn could take her place. It took a deep personal tragedy, necessitating a lengthy and expensive period spent eating fried chicken and apple sauce in a bleak little town in the Flevo area of the Netherlands, to rescue the horrified Dawn from losing her weekends and at least two evenings a week for the next two years. Sometimes less really is more.

VOLUNTEERMANSHIP

We move on now to consider another important, and sometimes overlooked, area of Stepmanship: Volunteermanship. Bearing in mind the experience of Dawn Cole, you may ask: Would it not be safer for Churchmen and women to volunteer for nothing?

There is some debate about the correct answer to this question, but I think it only right to quote Butterfield:

'The good Churchman will volunteer for *everything*.'[14]

Setting aside Butterfield's slight tendency towards exaggeration (less is always less and more is invariably even more than more in Butterfield's world), I have to say that we here at Churchmanship Headquarters would broadly agree with his view. Churchmen and

---

[14]   My italics

women would do well to become serial volunteers, thus acquiring the respect and admiration of the wider church community. How then, you will reasonably ask, does one avoid the morbid possibility of actually ending up doing the things that one has volunteered for? We would submit that close attention to our list of tips and guidelines will obviate most of these problems.

(a) Do your best to volunteer for tasks that have already been undertaken by someone else (*see addendum to Stepmanship concerning Stepping Up, above*).

(b) For goodness' sake be organized. Always check your diary before volunteering for any one-off activity to ensure that you will not be available on that day.

(c) Volunteer with pathetically wistful vim and gusto for jobs requiring skills and abilities in which you are seriously deficient. Lack of training or experience in electrical work and plumbing are particularly fruitful in this context. Always bear in mind, however, that there may be a labouring element to some of these tasks. Don't take the risk. Know before you go!

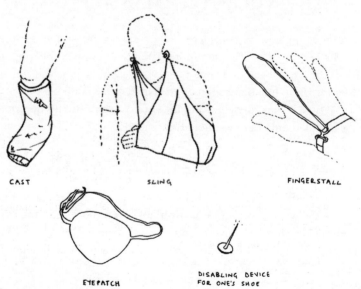

CAST

SLING

FINGERSTALL

EYEPATCH

DISABLING DEVICE
FOR ONE'S SHOE

(d) If you do decide to volunteer for practical or physical work in the church, find out what is required in advance and ensure that you arrive wearing a sling or a cast or a finger-stall, or an eyepatch or perhaps a disabling device in one shoe so that after you have offered your services with bright-eyed desperation someone has to kindly but firmly talk you out of taking part (*wide range of disabling props available from Churchmanship Headquarters at various competitive prices – see illustration*).

(e) The selective and sensitively infrequent use of phobias can be very helpful. Just about every task under the sun has its corresponding phobia, as we discovered after publishing an article in our last newsletter but three, in which we asked for the experiences of Churchmen and women in the use of this ploy. We include a selection of extracts from the replies we received for the interest and edification of our readers.

- Working in a small enclosed space such as a storage space under the church floor – claustrophobia
- Working in a church garden, graveyard or any other open space – agoraphobia
- Working in a dry, dusty loft or crypt – asthma/arachnophobia/amathophobia (fear of dust)
- Cleaning out some smelly old pond for the benefit of the community – hydrophobia (fear of water) or batrachophobia (fear of frogs, newts, etc.)
- Mending the church roof – hypsiphobia (fear of heights)
- Delivering meals to elderly foreign immigrants – xenophobia
- Attending the bishop's Lent course – porphyrophobia (fear of the colour purple)
- Helping with the youth group – ephebiphobia (fear of teenagers)
- Making up numbers for a prophetic macrame evening – linonophobia (fear of string)
- Undertaking car-park duties at a Christian event – motorphobia (fear of cars) and ichthyophobia (fear of fish)

- Attendance at meetings to discuss change – neophobia (fear of anything new)[15]
- Taking a group of lonely folk out for a meal at a Chinese restaurant – consecotaleophobia (fear of chopsticks)
- Helping with meals for anybody on any occasion – cibophobia (fear of food)
- Attending the mid-week prayer meeting – monophobia (fear of being alone)
- Helping at gospel outreach events – euphobia (fear of Good News)

Clearly, these and other phobias (*full list available from Churchmanship Headquarters, price three pounds including postage and packing*) should be used sparingly and with the finely polished veneer of intelligence that is expected from the best of our students. Dermot O'Brien of the Cornerstone Fellowship in Derry came close to ruining this fine ploy for all Churchmen and women when he made the absurd claim that he was suffering from panophobia (fear of everything). O'Brien subsequently became a Second Day Strict and Particular Baptist, discovering thereby that his ill-conceived ploy was a self-fulfilling prophecy.

(f) If ambushed or surprised by a request for assistance, we suggest bringing Provisionally-yesmanship into play. Procedure is straightforward. Gasp with incredulous delight at the prospect, assure the person who asked for your help that you are ninety-nine point nine per cent certain of being available, and rush excitedly off home to 'check the dates'. Later on the same evening you will need to make an appropriately devastated phone call, communicating in a very small voice that after desperately trying and failing to adjust events in your diary you have no choice but to pull out. The slightest hint of a sob is well worth considering.

---

[15] Unlikely to be very convincing in the context of Anglican or Methodist gatherings

In conclusion, it is important to emphasize the striking effects of properly executed Volunteermanship. Philip Ayreton, who infests a large Anglican church in Harborne near Birmingham, reports that he acquired a community-wide reputation for being 'willing and ready to lend a hand with whatever needs to be done'. This is a particularly remarkable achievement when you consider that, although Ayreton had volunteered for just about *everything*, he had never done *anything* – and it is a heart-warming endorsement of our Churchmanship motto, still carved in stone above the main entrance of our dear old Headquarters in Frome:

SITUS USUSFRUCTUM ADDIT[16]

---

[16] Idleness brings profit.

Section 7

DISTRACTMANSHIP

This year has seen a significant amount of good work continuing to be done in the important area of Distractmanship. This ploy, a crucial subdivision of Disconcertmanship (*see section on Disconcertmanship, below*), is the practice of putting off and generally distracting speakers and preachers. The last thing that Churchmen and women want is to be drawn into some dynamically genuine spiritual ethos or atmosphere. Well, what they say is true – prevention is better than cure. If the speaker can be successfully thrown off balance at an early stage in his or her talk, much that would be unwelcome can be avoided. I have listed below some of the most useful ploys known to us.

———— (1) THE NOTEBOOK PLOY ————

The Churchman or woman wishing to use this excellent ploy needs to remember two very important things.

First, it is essential to arrive early at the venue (wearing black-rimmed glasses and dressed, if possible, in the manner of a Further Education lecturer whose ambition is to be a writer) in order to occupy a seat that is on the front row and immediately in front of the spot where the speaker will stand.

Second, you will need to be equipped with a notebook, preferably the type known as a 'reporter's notebook', the pages of which turn on a spiral wire hinge, as well as a biro that has to be clicked with the thumb in order to reveal or enclose the nib (*special 'Pawker' pens available from Churchmanship Headquarters, each equipped with 'extra-loud click' technology at eight pounds per pen, including postage and packing – see illustration*).

You may execute phase one shortly before the preacher begins his talk. When he or she is looking in the general direction of the front row, take out your notebook, open it to a fresh page and balance it carefully on your knee. Just as the speaker begins his opening remarks take out your biro, click it into readiness (you should previously have adjusted click volume setting to '8' if using a Headquarters pen) and hold it poised for action immediately above your open notebook.

For phase two, study the speaker's face steadily and unsmilingly for a period of about two and a half minutes as he talks, then click the biro (volume adjusted to '10'), close your notebook and put pen and book away in an inside pocket. Lean back in your chair, place both hands behind your head, and glance to the left and to the right as though seeking a diversion of some kind. A small shake of the head and the faintest sigh of frustration can also be very helpful at this juncture.

So far we have heard nothing but praise for this exceptional ploy. C. Telfor, once of Glasgow, reports that one Church of Scotland minister was so taken aback by Telfor's huffing and puffing and pouting and dismissive posturing that he dropped his glasses, missed out points three, five, six and seven from his ten-point sermon and concluded with a summary of the lessons we might learn from a close study of encounters between Moses and God in the book of Revelation.

—— (2) THE WATCH-GLANCING PLOY——

There is, of course, an amazingly wide range of Watch-glancing Ploys. One of the best known is the eyes-dropped, rapid wrist revolution at waist level. We at Churchmanship Headquarters are happy to endorse this time-honoured practice, especially as it is the very (supposed) subtlety of the movement that is so infuriating to the speaker. For maximum effect, the good Churchman or woman will wait until a point in the talk at which the preacher *himself* believes that he is at his most moving or amusing or profound. This point is never difficult to spot as the person concerned will swell slightly and appear to gain extra physical stability. Nothing is more depressing for a speaker than to find, in the middle of his very best stuff, that a member of the congregation appears to be counting the minutes until his or her miserable ordeal is at an end.

—— (3) THE ENCOURAGEMENT PLOY——

It may seem ironic that Churchmanship Headquarters should support a negative concept such as encouragement, but as the large-jawed Butterfield[17] so rightly points out in his entertaining and instructive booklet 'Smiling with a Porpoise', the skilful use of this ploy can slow a speaker down almost to the point where he will come to a shuddering halt. Butterfield describes his technique with visiting preachers in customary detail.

---

[17] Butterfield's jaw is truly extraordinary. When he smiles his whole mouth seems to split and spread halfway round his head, not to mention the fact that he appears to have at least half as many teeth again as anyone else. Sometimes the smile is all that is needed. A visiting speaker who was preaching on 'Flowers of forgiveness rooted in the rich mulch of love' once confessed to me that a mere two minutes of this dolphin-like grin made him want to 'come down and hurt Butterfield very severely with something heavy and abrasive'.

I always make a point of getting to the venue in plenty of time to have a brief chat with the preacher before he begins. I clutch his upper arms tightly, look him very seriously in the eye and let him know that throughout his talk I shall be praying against *any repeat*[18] of the ill-mannered expressions of dissent and disagreement that we have recently experienced from one or two members of the congregation. I then wrinkle the whole of my face into a radiant, cabbage-like grin of encouragement and assure him that I will be right there on the front row offering support from the very first word he speaks until the very last.

This type of simple groundwork can sometimes be sufficient in itself to badly erode a speaker's confidence, but it is the second part of the ploy that delivers the *coup de grace*, as it were.

From the moment that the speaker opens his mouth I tuck my bottom lip between my teeth, fix a benevolent smile of appreciation and encouragement on my face, and begin the execution of a slow, rhythmic nodding movement of my head.

Points to bear in mind:

First, the rhythm and style of smiling and nodding should not alter one iota whether the speaker is telling a funny story or describing the death of his mother. I would go so far as to say that response must *never* connect with content. Bland, indiscriminate encouragement can drive a man almost to murder.

Secondly, experience and experiment suggest that in these circumstances a diagonal alignment of the head (*forty-seven degrees is the default angle in most ploys of this nature – see illustration*) is invariably more efficient than a vertical one. Why should this be the case? Who can tell? We must live in the mystery.

Thirdly, Venus Potterton, my last girlfriend but one, and a fine Churchwoman in her own right, asked a most insightful question. Why not, she suggested, add the Watch-glancing Ploy into the mix? Brilliant thinking.

---

[18]   My italics.

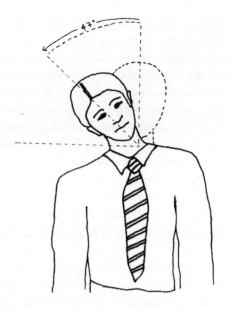

Our very next visiting speaker was a man named Lowell Chamberlain, a tall, blonde, confident man, who was coming to address us on the subject of Inner Serenity. By the time he reached the middle of his talk, my intensive, unremitting diagonal encouragement from the front row had, I think, already robbed him of any inner serenity that he might have had in the first place. And when, for one infinitesimal moment, I glanced down at my watch without even a miniscule interruption to the smiling and nodding, something seemed to snap inside Lowell. He paused for several seconds as though paralysed and then delivered the rest of his (shortened) talk directly to me in a weak, wistful, pleading voice.

I seem to recall he had to get someone to drive him home afterwards because he wasn't sure he could handle the steering.

Butterfield's specific use of encouragement in this context is constructive, and it clearly works, but bear in mind that encouragement does have a much wider application. This can, however, be taken too far. Sydney Adams, who (until the events we are about to describe) carried the banner of Churchmanship down in darkest Wiltshire, worked assiduously in the local New Frontiers church to which he once belonged to develop a reputation for having a *ministry of encouragement*. Results were dramatic but fatal to his future in that church. Sydney succeeded in persuading one young man that he was capable of undertaking interior decoration for a housebound member of the church. Not surprisingly, as the youth in question had never decorated so much as an iced bun in his life, the outcome was disastrous and had to be done all over again by someone who charged a fortune.

Sydney's greatest triumph (or disaster), however, and the situation in which he finally over-reached himself and was subsequently asked to exclude himself from the church, was a piano and violin concert performed one evening by two musically illiterate middle-aged ladies in the church hall. Over a lengthy period Sydney had challenged Miss Edwards and Miss Cornelius to exercise their belief that God is not restricted in the ways that men and women are restricted.

'What is the matter with us?' he would trumpet earnestly at them. 'Why do we limit God? The world says that you can't play musical instruments, simply because you have never learnt how to do it, but we are not of the world, are we? Are we? Well, are we? Come on! We know that anything is possible for those who truly believe. I want you to go into that hall and play by faith!'

On the evening of the performance quite a large number turned up for the concert, many of them intrigued to discover the existence of such unexpected talent in the church. As far as they knew or believed, Miss Edwards and Miss Cornelius had never mentioned or exhibited any interest or expertise pertaining to any musical instruments at all. Their belief was entirely justified. The noise made by the two maiden ladies as they plunged headlong into their duets from hell was breathtakingly dreadful. The audience suffered not only from the appalling cacophony, but also from having to make the terrible decision about whether to applaud or not at the end of each aural nightmare.

It was the end for Sydney. Like more than one incautious Churchman before him, he had taken a step too far. The church leaders ejected him. But he is a survivor. The last we heard of him, he was running prophetic break-dancing classes for disabled pensioners in Saffron Walden, thereby putting an even greater strain on the already stretched local health services.

(4) THE GETTING UP AND MOVING ABOUT PLOY

Churchmanship is very often about timing, and it is never more the case than in this ploy. Quite simply, it consists of leaving one's seat at a crucial point in the sermon or address (*see notes on Watch-glancing, above*) and moving around the church or hall in such a blatant manner as to distract the attention of all those present. The speaker is, in a sense, stranded – left to control feelings of impotent fury as he sees the eyes of his sheep-like listeners slide continually away from him as they fix on the cause of the commotion.

Opinions vary as to the best possible way of operating this ploy, but analysis suggests that two main strands have emerged in recent years. The first of these is the Elephantine Tiptoe, or ET, as it is known in Churchmanship circles. William Custer of Norwich, known affectionately as 'The General', has helpfully contributed a description of how he 'pulled an ET' in his own church last year.

The man who was doing the talk had been building up really well towards a climax, and I was watching and listening very carefully so as not to miss the best moment to deliver my ET. It came when he paused impressively after saying these stirring words.

'And so, dear friends, we come at last to the question that lies at the centre of all that we are and wish to be. And it is a question that I would like each one of you to ask in the next minute or two as we sit in silence and invite God to speak to us. The question is this . . .'

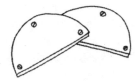

Wearing my heavy-duty black brogues with metal taps attached to toe and heel (*taps supplied by Churchmanship Headquarters, price twelve pounds per set including postage and packing – see illustration*), I rose from my seat and started to make my way past the front of the platform and down the central aisle through the middle of the congregation in the general direction of the toilets.

Naturally, I observed the primary rule of ET. *Do not hurry.* On the contrary, I employed an anguished, slow-motion, meticulously controlled mode of travel in which I held my arms high and lifted and lowered each foot with exaggerated care, as though desperate to avoid disrupting the meeting. In fact, of course, I achieved my real aim, which was to totally disintegrate the meeting. My bizarre, spidery progress through the church, punctuated by excruciating pauses before my metal taps hit the wooden floor each time I lowered a foot, easily secured the close attention of everyone in the church.

The speaker, reduced to lamely addressing the sides of people's heads until I had finally disappeared into the Gents, did his best to recover, but his neurotic concern that I was likely to re-emerge from the toilets at any moment must have been debilitating, to say the least.

Many thanks and congratulations to W. Custer. I should mention that the metal taps he mentions are not only available from Churchmanship Headquarters in children's sizes (*eight pounds per set, including postage and packing – see illustration for comparison with adult sets*) but are also already widely used throughout the United Kingdom, as can be heard and observed in a host of churches on almost any Sunday in the year.

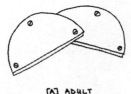
[A] ADULT

[B] CHILD

The second main strand in The Getting Up and Moving Around Ploy is known as The Highly Urgent Matter Ploy, or THUMP. It is true that THUMP and ET are similar in that both must be initiated at the worst possible time as far as the speaker is concerned, but THUMP is perhaps more suited to the younger, more active Churchman or woman capable of both suppleness and speed. For best results, operate the elements of the ploy in the prescribed order.

(a) At the commencement of the talk ensure that a small sheaf of printed papers is resting on your lap. Glance through the pile, nodding quietly and happily to yourself as though satisfied that arrangements and details have been properly dealt with. (The fact that you have had nothing whatsoever to do with the organization of the evening is, of course, irrelevant.)

(b) At that same carefully judged moment in the middle of the speaker's presentation, pull one of the sheets of paper from the stack and stare at it in alarm as though a glaring error or problem has suddenly come to light. Exhibit agitation. Rapid head-turning and knuckle chewing are recommended.

(c) Half rise from your seat and gaze around over the heads of the congregation, as though trying to spot the one person in the church who might be able to resolve your burning issue. Appear to suddenly locate this individual and wave your sheet of paper in the vague direction of the back row, signalling your intention of crossing the room to seek advice or consultation.

SHOE TAPS [ADULT]

(d) Leave your seat and, bent almost double at the waist (thus demonstrating your charitable desire to avoid blocking anyone's view or distracting attention from the message *see illustration*) make your way as briskly and urgently as your deformed shape will allow towards the back of the room. Choose a member of the congregation who is sitting in one of the least accessible seats and make your way to that person, hissing apologies to those you have to push past to get there.

When you arrive at the random person you have selected conduct a tense, whispered, one-sided conversation with them. Use such phrases as, 'Do you know who's responsible for this?' and jab worriedly with your index finger at the sheet of paper in your hand as you speak. The fact that the person involved will have not the slightest idea what is going on or what you are talking about is all to the good. His or her slight fear, concern and bewilderment can only amplify the sense of emergency that has been created.

(e) You may feel that, despite everything, the speaker is still holding his audience. If so, you should convey the impression through mime and gesture that the person you have buttonholed is indicating someone else in an equally inaccessible seat on the other side of the room who is *actually* the one capable of solving your problem. If your crashing, barging, loudly apologetic progress in the direction of your second innocent victim fails to have the desired effect you will know that you are dealing with someone less than or more than human (or possibly a highly skilled Churchman or woman), and you will be well advised to sit quietly at the back until the talk is finished.

(5) YAWNING PLOYS

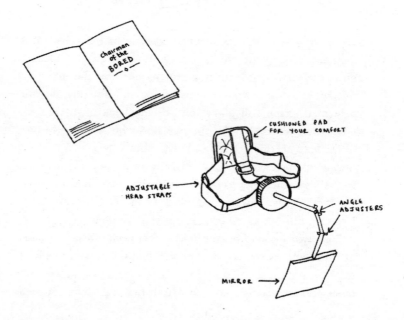

There are some who claim that yawning in the church is so wide-spread and common that it should not be regarded as a technical Churchmanship ploy. We are not in accord with this view. We believe that, properly understood and executed, Yawning remains one of the most useful tools at the disposal of those who are regularly engaged in Distractmanship.

Last spring we commissioned Esmond Perce[19] of Dorset, the acknowledged expert in this field, to produce a small booklet entitled 'Chairman of the Bored' (*available from Churchmanship Headquarters, price four pounds, fifty pence, or twenty pounds exactly with specially designed headclamp mirror, including postage and packing – see illustration*) in which the Yawning Ploys that he has developed over more than four decades are clearly categorized. We include three examples here. Practice is essential in all cases.

The Holding-it-in-at-All-Costs-Yawn

Churchmen and women should sit rigidly still and appear to be fighting to prevent their faces from revealing any trace of the

---

19 I cannot mention Esmond Perce without making reference to his excellent and undervalued Over the Shoulder Ploy. Here is Esmond's own description of the way in which it works.

Ideal in a crowded situation (during coffee-time after church, for instance) where it has become necessary to deflate or unsettle somebody else, I set this ploy in motion by deliberately engaging the person in conversation. After talking intensely and incessantly about myself for some minutes I stop and, with every appearance of being deeply interested, ask them a question about themselves (a favourite topic of conversation for ninety-nine percent of the population, Christian or otherwise). Once they are well launched into their answer and talking with real energy and concentration, I allow my eyes to drift away. I stare over one of their shoulders as though either I am hoping that a more interesting person might turn up or I am worried that I might miss someone more important.

Eventually, of course, the speaker will become aware that I am no longer listening, and his or her voice will dribble away, as it were, until I drag my attention back to what is being said and nod absent-mindedly. After that, simply repeat the process as required. It is guaranteed to annoy at the very least, in virtually every case.

yawn that is threatening to convulse them. Bulging eyes, as well as expanding, contracting and twisting facial muscles and restrained but unmistakeable air-sucking noises indicate clearly that a major yawn is definitely in progress (*see illustration*).

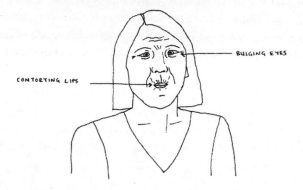

The Just-Thought-of-Something-Interesting-Yawn

Once again, the aim is to increase the negative effect of the yawn by appearing to conceal it. In this ploy the eyes are rolled towards the ceiling as though an idea has suddenly occurred to the Churchman or woman, and the whole of one hand is placed across the open mouth at an angle of forty-seven degrees, as if in contemplation. Reveal yawn through fingers as appropriate (*see illustration*).

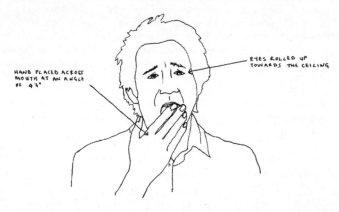

The Back-Row-Blow-out-Yawn

This much cruder variety of Yawning Ploy might best be regarded as a final (but usually very successful) resort. Best executed on the back row of a church or hall, it involves the gradual disappearance of the yawner as he or she engages the entire body and both arms and legs in one lengthy, unrestrained, groaning, gasping, gaping, voluptuous, energy-consuming yawn. While it can have a slam-dunk effect on a speaker's confidence, it is less than subtle in Churchmanship terms (*see illustration*).

The Nodding-into-Unconsciousness-Ploy

This is not technically a yawn, but it is a strikingly successful initiative, calling for considerable acting skill on the part of the practitioner.

The ploy is begun by nodding slowly, seriously and encouragingly as the speaker begins to make his points. Five minutes of such consistently and clearly signalled agreement should ensure that the majority of the talk is now being addressed directly to the Churchman. It is time for phase two of the ploy.

The nodding motion of the head should be gradually regulated until it becomes continuous and metronomically rhythmic, while the lower jaw is made to drop seven centimetres (*see illustration*). Allow the eyes to become glazed and let the eyelids droop, close and spring open again. Repeat this pattern until the talk ends and the congregation is called to prayer. At the point when the speaker says, 'Let us bow our heads in prayer', the churchman's mechanically-nodding head should drop towards his knees like a concrete ball falling from a gatepost, an indication that blessed sleep has finally been allowed to release him from the struggle. Three seconds should be left after the final 'Amen' before suddenly springing upright, arms waving and eyeballs rolling wildly in confusion.

It is a good plan to apologize sheepishly to the distressed speaker afterwards, making some feeble excuse about being up late the night before. Being in Christian Speaker Mode, he will almost certainly laugh and say that he would have fallen asleep himself if he had been in the congregation, or some such nonsense. But make no mistake – he will hate you.

——(6) SILENT BUT DEADLY APPLAUSE—— AND UNWANTED WATER

Elton Spalling of the Living Light Fellowship in Portishead writes to offer members the use of two ploys that he has found consistently useful in his dealings with visiting speakers over the years.

Spalling claims that short bursts of silent applause from a point at the side of the church that is only just inside the speaker's line of sight, especially when accompanied by a strangely twisted and knowing smile, can reduce a sermon or message by fifty per cent or more. This has provoked at least one man into punching the lectern by mistake and having to suck his hand until the pain eased.

His second ploy involves hurrying out quite unnecessarily to fetch a glass of water for the speaker in the middle of his talk, and rushing it up to the lectern with the bustling urgency that would be appropriate for a man who is having a choking fit. Once, Spalling reports, he physically pinched the speaker's nose and poured water into his mouth as he gasped for air. Whilst applauding the determination and commitment demonstrated by this latter ploy, we are obliged to observe that attempting to solve the problem of visiting speakers by drowning them fails to achieve the standards of subtlety that we expect from our members. Spalling is young. He will learn.

───── (7) OPPORTUNISMANSHIP ─────

No discussion of Distractmanship would be complete without pointing out the necessity for Churchmen and women to take advantage of unexpected chances when they arise. After all, random opportunities can be seized and replicated in the future. Paul Winston of Macclesfield has furnished us with an example of Opportunismanship at its best.

> There was a visiting speaker called Norman Fellot at our church one Sunday, one of those very laid-back, confident men with humorous eyes, a disproportionately expensive brown leather briefcase and an air of conditional goodwill. He was from one of those charities that send people round to raise awareness and money and that kind of thing. Conscious that his presence was likely to disturb the unruffled, harmless ethos of our Baptist assembly, you may readily imagine that I was on the lookout for any means by which I might be able to offset the danger.

My chance came when I went up to the central lectern to read the Bible passage for that morning (I had done a deal with a tearfully grateful June Pargitter whereby I would perform this task in her place so that she could visit a sick friend, and in exchange she would take on my next six tasks in the church, whatever they happened to be).

On reaching the front I discovered that Fellot had placed the notes for his talk on the lectern, ready for when he came up after I had finished the reading. Glancing at the top page as I lowered my *large* Bible,[20] I realized that Fellot's talk was printed out word for word on several sheets of thin paper, with what appeared to be little pencilled asides and jokes in the margins.

When I picked up my Bible after completing the reading I made sure that I also accidentally picked up all of Fellot's notes and carried them carefully back to my place on the back row, where it was the work of a moment to screw them into a ball and push them into the bottom of what I call my 'Sunday Sack'.

Fellot did his best, but it might have been better if he had admitted that his notes had gone missing. After his first goggle-eyed, panic-stricken attempts to physically pick up something that simply wasn't there, he stumbled his humourless way through ten minutes or so of waffle before returning with perspiration and relief to his seat on the front row. By craning my neck I could see him from where I was, burrowing through his briefcase and inside jacket pockets with restrained wildness while trying to give the appearance of still paying attention to the rest of the service.

On leaving, his creased brow and hunted expression bore witness to Fellot's continued preoccupation with the sheer

---

[20] Paul Winston is yet another of those happy members who have taken advantage of the opportunity to purchase one of our Full-works De Luxe Bibles (*see section on Bibles, below*)

impossibility of what had happened. As he walked out of the door, I glanced at one of the stewards and raised my eyebrows in a 'We don't judge, but my goodness, whatever do you make of all that, then?' sort of way. He shook his head slowly from side to side in response. The whole thing was a great success, and I offer it as a possible ploy to be used and adapted by members in the future.

Custer and Staveling

William Custer (*see Section 4 on Church of Englandmanship, above*) is another fine exponent of Opportunismanship, sometimes going to enormous lengths in order to achieve small but significant results. There was the notable occasion, for instance, when Custer had decided that Major General Sir Gerald Staveling, one of the wardens in Custer's church (St Stephen in Rustbury and Gateland in Suffolk) had acquired too firm a grip over just about every aspect of church life. Custer was of the opinion that the best way to profoundly disconcert the very correct and never flippant old soldier was to somehow make him *appear* flippant in an entirely inappropriate context.

His chance came when Staveling was due to read the lesson on one Remembrance Sunday in the late nineties. Having established which passage was to be read, Custer acquired a key to St Stephen's and locked himself in on the Saturday night before the service with a packet of white-tack, some cigarette papers and an artist's pen. Fifteen minutes of painstaking work saw the job done, and it was with a sense of lively anticipation that Custer took his seat on the Sunday morning and awaited the moment when the Major General would march stiffly up to the lectern and begin his reading.

The result was all that he could have hoped for. Major General Staveling was not a reflective man, and the very idea of someone tampering with the reading was beyond his imagination or comprehension.

On arriving at the front of the church he took his rigidly military stance behind the lectern and addressed the congregation in the barking, monotonous tones of one who has been reading lessons from the King James Version in country churches since time began.

'The lesson on this very special day may be found on page eight hundred and eighteen of your pew Bible, and is taken from the Gospel of Saint Matthew, the sixteenth chapter, and verses thirteen to nineteen. Our Lord enquires of Peter who he believes him to be.'

Staveling woofed his way through verses thirteen to seventeen in the satisfyingly hollow but harmless way associated with all such readings in such places. It was in verse eighteen that he heavily and unsuspectingly trod on Custer's carefully buried verbal landmine. These were the words the congregation heard.

'And I say also unto thee, that thou art Hank, and upon this rock I will build my church; and the gates of hell will not prevail against it.'

Staveling ploughed on through the concluding verse, though his purple face and bulging eyes indicated that he must have been aware of the congregation's response to the surprising assertion by Holy Scripture that Jesus might have entrusted the future of his entire church to someone called 'Hank'. A few were choked with mirth, clearly feeling that the gates of hell would be onto a good thing in these particular circumstances. Far more, including the minister, were amazed, appalled, affronted and probably lots of other similar words beginning with 'a' that a man of such stature as the Major General should have seen fit to indulge in such a childishly trivial and pointless piece of so-called humour.

Staveling, who obviously felt that a resourceful officer like himself should be able to rescue the situation even in the midst of battle, dug his grave a little deeper by making a public announcement.

'This is the word of the Lord. Well – one of them is not. I feel I should make it clear that Our Lord did not, despite what this Bible says, at any time include in the body of his believers a man whose name was Hank. Hurrumph!'

Afterwards, Major General Staveling protested stoutly, but with a certain wildness in his eyes, that he had read the words exactly as they appeared in the church Bible. However, as Custer had carefully removed the slip of cigarette paper from page eight hundred and eighteen as soon as possible after the end of the service, his claim was received with concern from some and disapproval from others.

Staveling's grip on church affairs was significantly loosened from that point onwards, and Custer was quietly proud.[21]

———(8) POOR TASTEMANSHIP———

We conclude our section on Distractmanship by mentioning the good work done in the area of Poor Tastemanship by Ewan Barret of Sompting in Sussex. Here is an extract from his latest report.

There is nothing more vexing for a visiting Christian speaker than to be thought guilty of poor taste. I offer this ploy as one that I have tested and found extremely efficacious.

Greet your visiting speaker warmly when he arrives and offer him a piece of paper on which is written a relatively lengthy joke that will 'go down particularly well with our people here' if he would care to use it. Let us say that the joke ends with a punchline involving a bus or, better still, a person being run over by a bus. Assuming that the speaker decides to use the joke with which you have so generously furnished him, choose a moment when he is on the verge of reading the punchline, then hurry to the front and hand him a note. This will advise him that someone whose mother was run over by

---

[21] Custer reports that, for a period of some weeks, children who had attended the Remembrance service delighted in telling each other that one of Jesus' disciples had been known as Hank Hurrumph.

a bus eighteen months ago has unexpectedly turned up in the church and would be devastated to hear this particular joke at a time when she is still grieving.

The last time that I used this ploy the speaker hurriedly adapted his joke so that it ended with a person almost being slightly grazed by a passing moped, thus rendering the joke totally meaningless.

Ewan Barret is, of course, famous in Churchmanship circles for the evening when he offered another, quite different, joke to an after-dinner speaker at a joint-churches occasion held at the Wolfenden Rooms in Sompting. This story concerned the origin of the name 'Sompting'. Unfortunately for the speaker, he was not aware that various tensions surrounding this issue had recently come close to creating conflict among local churches.

The joke, told with terrible confidence by the grateful visiting speaker, surmised that in years past a meeting had been held to decide the name of the town. After much wearying and fruitless debate an Irishman, exploding with impatience, cried, 'Begorrah, we've got to cawl it sompting!' And that, concluded the speaker, was exactly what they did.

The silence that ensued, reports Barret, was as chilled and endless as the eternally drifting ice floes of the Arctic.

Section 8
THUMBNAIL THEOLOGY

Thumbnail Theology offers a variety of ways for Churchmen and women to give the impression of having profound and widespread knowledge in the field of theology without having to go through the tedious and unproductive business of studying the subject.

————THE ONE INTELLIGENT———— QUESTION PLOY

This interesting and well developed sub-ploy was designed and developed by Christopher Carter of Dursley in Gloucestershire. It is Carter's contention that if the Churchman is willing and able to learn one intelligent question by heart, he will be fully equipped to emerge from theological debate with a genuine theologian looking and sounding as if he is by way of being something of an expert himself.

'Pick your moment carefully,' advises Carter, 'and then introduce your question in as humble a manner as possible. After that all you have to do is nod and shake your head a bit. From time to time it could be a good idea to look as if you might have been tempted to disagree, but have thought better of it on reflection.'

Carter quotes an occasion when a visiting speaker delivered a lecture on the German theologian Rudolf Bultmann in the church hall one evening. Knowing what the subject was to be, Carter had spent part of that morning learning a quotation from the internet. When the speaker asked for questions at the end of his speech, the Churchman was ready:

CARTER: (*wringing his hands together nervously*) Look, I'm a complete blockhead when it comes to theology, my friend, but seeing as you obviously know your way around with all this stuff, there is one damn fool question I'd really like to ask if you don't mind.

EXPERT: No, no, of course I don't mind. Go ahead.

CARTER: Well, I'd just like to know if you agree with Pawlikowski that within Christian biblical scholarship the dominance of the '*Religionsgeschite*' approach, obviously found in Rudolph Bultmann especially but also some of his disciples such as Ernst Kasemann and Helmut Kosester, has significantly receded. Silly schoolboyish question, I know, but I'd just love to hear your view on that.

EXPERT: (*hugely pleased and surprised*) No, no, it's a very good question. This was the view expressed by Pawlikowski in *Reflections on Covenant and Mission Forty Years after Nostra Aetate*, wasn't it?

CARTER: (*considering for a moment then nodding sagely*) Yes, yes, I believe it was. Yes, I think you're right there.

EXPERT: Well, I have to say that I think Pawlikowski went a little too far –

CARTER: Ah, *do* you? Too far? Now that *is* interesting.

EXPERT: Well, you may disagree with me, for reasons that you and I are all too aware of –

CARTER: Oh, good Lord, yes!

EXPERT: But the crucial point, one you will readily understand, is that Bultmann was, in the final analysis . . . etc., etc.

Carter reports that other members of the church were greatly impressed by such unexpected erudition, despite his continually expressed, self-effacing assertion that he had only ever skimmed the surface of theology in general and Bultmann in particular.

─────────── BIOGRAPHICAL BITES ───────────

Churchwoman Dawn Cole (*see Section 6 on Stepmanship, above*) is far less interested in impressing expert theologians than in developing ways to interrupt and disturb their natural flow. To this end she advocates a slightly different approach to Thumbnail Theology, favouring a sub-ploy known as Biographical Bites. Dawn believes that a small, obscure detail from the life of a theologian, dropped into the conversation more or less at random, can put the most confident and fluent expert off his stroke.

She describes, for instance, a Bible study meeting in someone's sitting room where a man called Paul Vann, a university professor from Hull who really did know a great deal about Martin Heidegger, was holding forth in a truly interesting and apparently unstoppable way. Dawn was in possession of one very small fact about the great German theologian and philosopher, but she used it with great skill.

VANN: The thing we need to understand about Heidegger is his contention that Western philosophy since Plato has misunderstood what it means for something to be, tending to approach this question in terms of *a* being, rather than asking about being itself. In other words, he believed that all investigations of being have historically focussed on particular entities and their properties, or they have treated being itself as an entity, or substance, with properties. Now, a more authentic analytic of being would, for Heidegger, investigate –

DAWN: So much time spent in that isolated mountain hut. What does an experience like that do to a man?

VANN: I'm sorry?

DAWN: Heidegger. All on his own in that little hut. How would that have affected his thinking, I wonder?

VANN: Well, yes, I suppose –

DAWN: It was at Todtnauberg, wasn't it?

VANN: Todtnauberg.

DAWN: Yes, up in the mountains. So isolated.

VANN: Yes . . .

DAWN: What must that have done to Heidegger, I wonder? To his thinking. The isolation, I mean. Just a little hut. Todtnauberg is so very isolated.

VANN: Yes . . .

Vann completely lost his drift after that and the ensuing discussion, a very animated one, revolved around the type, size and function of sheds and summerhouses owned by members of the Bible study group and their relatives and friends. Vann confessed worriedly to having no shed of any description.

Dawn Cole has kindly offered to make her full list of Biographical Bites available to members (*complete list available from Churchmanship Headquarters, price two pounds including postage and packing*). They include such useful items of information as the fact that Karl Barth was married to a very talented violinist; that Soren Kierkegaard's mother was a maid in the Kierkegaard's family home before marrying Soren's father, Michael Pederson Kierkegaard; and that Martin Luther described the university he attended at Erfurt as a beerhouse and a whorehouse. All of these, says Dawn, are little nuggets that will prove most valuable when used properly, and they are almost certainly all you will ever need to know about those theologians.

—— THE IMAGINARY THEOLOGIAN ——

Members will not be at all surprised to hear that one of the boldest and most innovative practitioners in this field is Julius Butterfield, who has actually *invented* a German theologian named Venktmann.

'I can't help asking myself what Venktmann would have to say about all this,' he will murmur calmly and reflectively in the middle of a heated discussion on some theological point.

'Venktmann has one or two quite startling things to say on this topic,' is another of his favourites.

And, perhaps most useful of all: 'That's interesting. How would you reconcile that view with Venktmann's comments on the same subject?'

When asked who Venktmann is Butterfield will reply shyly, 'Venktmann? Oh, good heavens, he's just an obscure little German theologian, but he does seem to talk an awful lot of sense. People like

Barth and Bultmann occupy an important place. Of course they do. But you can give me Venktmann every time – perhaps because he's a very clever man with an enormous breadth of knowledge who never speaks down to people like me, the ordinary little person in the pew. Where does he stand as a theologian and philosopher? Well, I suppose if you pushed me into a corner and poked me with a sharp stick, I'd have to say that he tends to bridge the gap between postmodernism and existential psychology, if that makes sense. A bit simplistic, I know, but I guess you'd have to place him somewhere there.'

The benefits of having your own tame theologian are obviously immense. Venktmann's views on just about everything were, and are (unsurprisingly), extremely close to those held by Butterfield himself. Now and then folk will ask if they can borrow a book by the obscure theologian, but it appears that Venktmann's works are out of print, and as Butterfield's copies are rare and fragile, they cannot be allowed to leave the house. He will, very rarely, copy out a paragraph or a page and lend it to those who are truly interested. They are most grateful.

JUNG AT HEART

It is interesting to note that Dawn Cole was mentored and privately tutored in Churchmanship by Berkeley Travis, who was known throughout churches in the north of England as an expert on the relationship between Christianity and the teaching of Carl Jung, even though he never once addressed any group or gathering on that subject and knew very nearly nothing about Jung. Travis was a highly skilled operator, and it was my privilege to see him, many years ago, at work in the back room of the Anglican Church of St James near the centre of Cockermouth in Cumbria.

Biding his time until someone made a fairly harmless comment about the way in which archetypal Anglicanism has changed over the last twenty years, he suddenly fell back in his chair, waving his legs in the air and guffawing loudly.

'Let the post-Jungians pick the bones out of that!' he spluttered, apparently wiping tears of laughter from his eyes with a large yellow handkerchief dragged from a deep trouser pocket.

To my certain knowledge, Travis had no idea who or what post-Jungians might be, nor why this obscure category of persons might want to pick the bones out of anything at all, let alone the innocuous comment that had just been passed. One timid soul did venture to ask how Jung was relevant to Anglicanism.

'He was an analytical psychologist!' replied Travis with sudden, brusque fierceness, as though that fact in itself was a sufficient and indisputable answer to the question.

When there was a further query as to how Jung would tackle the concept of Anglican stereotypes, Travis did not hesitate for an instant.

'Abstract and express,' he replied briskly, 'that is what he would advise us to do initially. Abstract and express. He would see it as a matter of fundamental contextualism. You see, Jung was contextual by nature. Yes, by nature. I would go further and say that he was bi-contextual, and I think I would need to add that he was synchronistic in focus. After all, we must constantly bear in mind that Carl Jung had been a very solitary and introverted child who grew up with a view of women as being innately unreliable.'

Travis's use of this one actual piece of knowledge about Jung leaves us in no doubt that Dawn Cole owes her concept of Biographical Bites, at least in part, to this great Churchman. Often invited to deliver talks on various aspects of Jung, Travis invariably refused, saying that:

'The attractive presentation of a philosophy disguised as a psychological model is unlikely to be helpful in the integration of spirituality and in the appreciation of unconscious realms.'

Those who had invited him to their churches usually nodded ruefully on hearing this, as though Travis's point was an obvious one they hadn't thought of, and they replied that they understood perfectly.

Interestingly, the renowned Churchman came to look more and more like Carl Jung as he grew older. This was achieved and fostered by Travis himself, who by a tremendous shaving and dying and fluffing of the hair at the sides of his head, and by losing weight and wearing unnecessary spectacles and learning to smoke a pipe, came to bear an uncanny likeness to the Swiss psychiatrist. We shall not see his like again.

—————————— PENDULUM PLOYS ——————————

In this fascinating area of theological Churchmanship it is essential to remember that a little knowledge does enable one to profoundly influence the tides of theological opinion. Churchmanship students are frequently surprised to learn that we as a movement feel deeply indebted to Martin Luther for his contribution to theological understanding. This is especially so in the sense that the doctrine of salvation by grace is commonly and mistakenly regarded by Churchmen and non-Churchmen alike as being in some vague sense diametrically opposed to the divine requirement for good works in the lives of believers.

Naturally, we do not expect our students to become bogged down in the detail of all this (indeed, the second chapter of Ephesians and the entire book of James are required non-reading on all of our courses). However, the faith/works illusion is extremely useful to Churchmen and women in many contexts, and particularly as it broadens out into the crucial and fruitful area of Pendulum Ploys. Some of the most successful of these are explained below.

The Basic Grace/Works Pendulum Ploy

Keen Churchmen and women will always be watching the way in which the pendulum is swinging in their church, and it is between the phantom poles of Grace and Works that this is most likely to happen. Jeremy Gates-Pound of Gloucestershire is a Churchman of vast experience, and the originator of the Worried Head-scratching Sub-ploy, or WHSS, that has been used with such sparkling results by literally hundreds of our members.

Gates-Pound makes the point (a remarkably philosophical one for a Churchman) that at any given time all church communities are swinging towards an emphasis either on a state of Being or a state of Doing. It is, says Gates-Pound, the responsibility of the Churchman to accurately judge the point at which this oscillation can be halted or reversed by proper use of the WHSS or its variants. The aim always is to prevent the church (a) from moving too far towards either end of the spectrum, and (b) from embracing the theological truth that wherever Grace has genuinely planted faith it is inevitable that good works will be generated. Far from being opposites, Grace and Works are supposed to be, as it were, two sides of the same coin.[22] The grasping of this latter truth by any church is not good news for Churchmen or women. Hence, the importance of this ploy.

Let Gates-Pound himself describe its execution.

'I first discovered the power of the WHSS when I had managed to get myself onto something called the "Vision and Strategy Group" (VAST for short) at an Anglican church in the little village of Cornford in Kent, midway between Ashford and Canterbury. Eight of us met one Wednesday morning at my house (*strategic* on my part, as it was likely to fulfil my *vision* of achieving more leverage, if you get my drift) to discuss ways in which we as a church could show care for the neighbourhood

---

[22] It is important to point out here a significant difference between the groundwork of Gates-Pound and that of Steadman in his strategy regarding congregation-swivelling plans (*see section on Special Relationshipmanship, above*). Steadman *distanced* himself. Gates-Pound *ingratiated* himself. Useless to make comparisons here. Better to remember the words of the late Vernon Poole, poet of Churchmanship:

Two Ploysters, braced in common fight,
One shall stand in darkness, one in light.
And who shall say that he is wrong, or she is right,
Unless they see and know the victim's plight?

By all means make a close study of either of these great exponents of Churchmanship, but remember that they both have much to offer.

by offering practical help and assistance on a regular basis. Naturally this prospect troubled me, and I had spent part of the previous evening working out a plan of action for the next morning. These were the elements of my plan (*see diagrams*):

(1) I deliberately did not shave that morning.

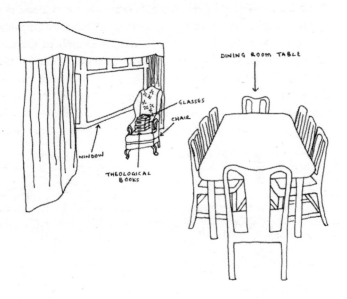

(2) I decided that the meeting should take place around my dining-room table in order to invest the gathering with a more formal, committee-like atmosphere.

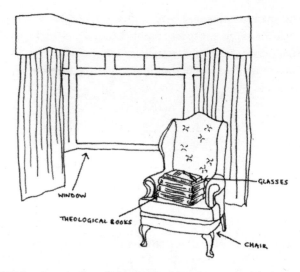

(3) I left a large pile of theological books on the chair next to
the window on the long side of the table with my glasses
balanced on top so that they would be visible to all, and so
that no one else would be able to sit there.

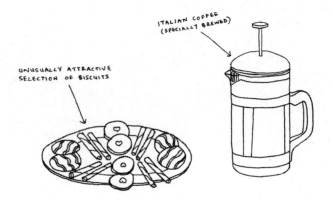

(4) I bought an unusually attractive selection of biscuits for
everyone to eat with specially brewed rich Italian coffee and
a choice of first-rate decaff.

(5) Before anyone arrived I tousled my hair in an attractively scruffy way, undid the top button of my shirt and skewed my tie to the left after loosening the knot (*see illustration*).

When the others arrived I welcomed them with a sweet, weary smile, plied them with steaming coffee (choice of normal or decaff as indicated above), a small glass of iced water, and mixed chocolate biscuits. I also enquired earnestly after their families. As the formal discussion began I continued to smile and nod at each person who spoke,[23] but said nothing.

At last a moment came when it felt right to carry out the first part of my major ploy.

Swinging impetuously round and allowing my arm to hang down and swing over the back of my chair, I threw my head back in Byronic fashion and gazed out of the window, as if glimpsing the shape of some great, shining truth far, far away up in the sky.

---

[23]   Three-week 'Smiling and Nodding' courses available each autumn at Church-manship Headquarters.

Turning and recovering myself with a little smile of apology I then gave my full, rapt attention to Phyllis Denham, who was talking with such logic and passion that it became necessary to pass the plate of biscuits in her direction and spill one or two clumsily in front of her as she spoke in order to interrupt her flow and continue the momentum of my ploy.

Finally, instinctively, I knew that the moment had come for the execution of the WHSS proper. Leaning my elbows down on the table in front of me, I lowered my head and scrubbed and scratched busily at the centre parting of my hair whilst secretly imparting increased bleariness to my eyes with my two smallest fingers (*see illustration*) until someone said, 'Something up, Jez?'

Surfacing slowly, I smiled a crumpled, bleary smile around the table before speaking.

'No, I'm fine, honestly. It's just that I was awake through most of the night, thinking – praying, you know how it is. Doing a spot of reading.'

I slightly self-consciously patted the top of the pile of theology books beside me as I said this.

'I tell you what, folks, I'm just a little bit worried about the direction we're going in – but maybe this isn't the right time for . . .'

Full of my coffee, biscuits and general hospitality everyone hastened to assure me that this *was* the right time.

'Well, I suppose it's just that I'm feeling very happy about what we do, what we're planning to do, all that stuff, but I'm not half as sure about – well, about what we *are*. We do these things because we are – what? I think that's important and I don't know if you agree with me, but I would hate it to get lost in all the busyness and the doing. I wouldn't want it to get crowded out. You tell me. Am I being foolish here? (*a little self-deprecating chuckle works wonders at this point*) I do talk a load of rubbish when I'm tired sometimes.'

But no, it transpired that I was not being foolish, and that every-one agreed with me that we would hate whatever-it-was to get lost in whatever-the-other-thing-was, and that perhaps we should draw back a little and just make sure that we were etc., etc.'

Textbook Churchmanship by Gates-Pound, and it is valuable to point out the truth that undergirds this fine ploy. Namely, that it is almost always possible to stop a church in its tracks by suggesting that the time has come to 'redefine our spiritual identity and the true nature of our mission'. Experience shows that a full six months of inactivity can be achieved as this virtually impossible task is being attempted. Church people tend to be nervous and tentative in this area. Failure to exploit this fact would be a real sin.

Oscar Wildemanship – Wisdom in the Church

Oscar Wildemanship is simply a subdivision of Pendulum Ploy and a variation on Elaine Broadwater's discovery of the power of opposites. It provides an easy way for even the densest and most obtuse Churchman or woman to give an impression of great wisdom in the church context. The title of the ploy originated in one of those rare moments of inspiration when veteran Churchman J.V. Toll of Broadstairs found himself staring at a coffee mug standing on the kitchen windowsill of his home. On the side of the mug was printed a quote from Oscar Wilde, a poet and playwright who, in this modern age, would certainly have risen with lightning speed through the ranks of the Churchmanship movement. Toll's mug bore the brief legend:

'Only dull people are brilliant at breakfast.'
—Oscar Wilde

Two thoughts flashed upon Toll with the vividness of divine revelation. One was the fact that this typical Wildeism would be no less profound if the words 'dull' and 'brilliant' were exchanged.

'Only brilliant people are dull at breakfast'
—J.V. Toll

As we have already seen with the interchange of Christian terms (*see section on Pulpy Wordmanship, above*), there are endless possibilities in this area. But it was the second point that inspired Toll. Could it be, he asked himself, that it is only necessary for the ambitious Churchman or woman to employ opposites in the context of paradox in order to give an appearance of wisdom bordering on the mystical? After considerable experiment and research he discovered that this was indeed the case, and the fruits of his labours are now available for use by members.

Toll maintains that, used appropriately, these startling truisms are capable of bringing discussions and Bible studies to a complete halt as people struggle to, as Toll himself puts it, 'unstick the concepts like chewing gum from the insides of their minds'. See the examples below (*full list available from Churchmanship Headquarters, price two pounds fifty pence including postage and packing*).

(1) The man who accepts all has rejected everything, but he who accepts nothing will be rejected by all those who have accepted everything.

(2) Only a person completely devoid of faith can begin to know what it means to believe.

(3) We shall not find God until we finally accept that we have lost him.

(3a) We shall not lose God as long as we accept that we have never found him.

(4) It is by walking willingly into the darkest cloud that we shall see clearly for the first time.

(5) We will only genuinely learn to love and not hate if we learn to hate the lack of love in us and in others, to love the lack of hate in others and in us, to love the love in us and in others and to hate the hate that is in others and in us when love is not in us and in others.

(6) You may be sure that when God speaks from immediately behind us he is directly in front of us, and when he speaks from in front of us he is invariably behind us.[24]

(7) In the centre of darkness we discover light, and that light is the true heart of darkness, just as the heart of light is the darkest place we shall ever know.

(8) It is in leaving that we shall stay, in striving that we shall rest, in destroying that we shall build, in weeping that we shall be glad, in eating that we shall starve, in fasting that we shall be fed and in joy that we shall know the deepest meaning of sorrow.

(9) Spin the coin of heaven and hell by all means, but remember that when it lands it will always be the obscured side that is visible.

---

[24] Despite this extraordinary picture of God inexplicably revolving round and round those he is speaking to like Norman Wisdom on speed, Toll reports that this piece of 'wisdom' was more solemnly and reverentially received than almost any other. This is more often the case than one might think. Churchman Simeon Veil of Peel, on the Isle of Man, was in the habit of stating that:

'Grace and Law are not bedfellows, they are walking companions.'

This sort of nonsensical drivel produced very positive responses from those who were, in just about all other circumstances, perfectly rational.

(10) The man who would draw near to God must learn to hear through his eyes, smell through his ears and see through his nose.

Section 9
USING TECHNOLOGY FOR THE LORD-MANSHIP

In this exciting new section of our special anniversary report we are delighted to highlight additional essential and cutting-edge products to be used in the service of a range of Churchmanship ploys. We look forward to hearing how you, our agents in the field, expand on the possibilities of Using Technology for the Lord-manship. We begin, of course, with the Bible.

─────── CHURCHMANSHIP AND ─────── THE BIBLE

It has sometimes been claimed by those who know nothing of Churchmanship that we are in some way against the Bible. Nothing could be farther from the truth. Here at Headquarters we have consistently advocated that Churchmen and women should pay special attention to the type of Bible that they own and the way in which they use it. Because this is such an important issue, we have designed a range of Bibles for sale to members. We have listed some of these Bibles, with illustrations, below.

The Full-works De Luxe
We are modestly proud of our Full-works De Luxe, a Bible constructed here in our own workshops and available exclusively from Churchmanship Headquarters (*ninety-five pounds per Bible including postage and package – see illustration*). This splendid, satchel-sized Bible is individually constructed, personally thumbed, tastefully stained, decorated with over five hundred post-it bookmarks, and marked throughout with genuinely handwritten, annotated notes. Each volume

also comes equipped with specially reinforced flexible covers designed to flop impressively over both sides of one hand, leaving the Churchman or woman free to gesture and gesticulate with the other as he or she addresses churches or small groups.

Two recent testimonials convey the satisfaction experienced by those who have purchased this product.

> I have never read the Bible, and now I probably never will. I don't need to. The Full-works De Luxe takes all the hard work out of developing a Bible to be proud of. My copy has been admired and commented on by many people in the church that I attend. Keep up the good work(s).
>
> —Velma Smart, Rugby

I have gone from being regarded as a spiritual pygmy to acquiring a reputation as a spiritual giant, and I owe it all to the Full-works De Luxe. Thank you especially for the handwritten note in Isaiah about my very moving personal epiphany, and for the tear stains in the thirteenth chapter of Corinthians about love. I don't know how you do it for the money!

–Philip Underside, Pulborough

The Miracle Midget Bible with Optional Pince-nez or Magnifying Glass

Our delightful Miracle Midget Bible (*twelve pounds fifty pence; sixteen pounds with pince-nez; fifteen pounds with magnifying glass, postage and packing included – see illustration*) is specifically intended as a counter-ploy to those who own a genuine version of the Full-works De Luxe. Measuring only two-and-a-half inches square, this perfect miniature contains all sixty-six books of the Bible and is small enough to be contained in most inside jacket pockets and all handbags.

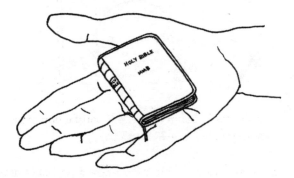

The Midget, as we affectionately refer to it here at Headquarters, is designed as an aid to the execution of Bumbling Goodwillmanship and is best employed in a jovially innocent, disorganized manner. Done properly, an embarrassed fumbling through bulging pockets or rubbish-filled handbags for the miniscule Bible, and then for pince-nez or magnifying glass, creates a sense of simple faith and endearing ordinariness that is more than a match for those who insist on displaying larger and more sophisticated versions of Scripture.

The optional use of pince-nez is a little stroke of genius by Vernon Mann of Dudley, who reported that, although his sight is perfectly good, the use of pince-nez (with clear glass, of course) added a certain Dickensian quirkiness to his performance (*see illustration*). Others favour the magnifying glass, enabling as it does a mole-like peering vulnerability that radiates childlike humility.

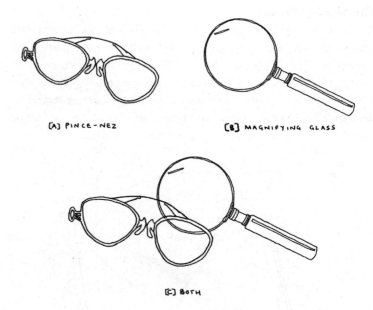

[A] PINCE-NEZ

[B] MAGNIFYING GLASS

[C] BOTH

The testimonial printed below reached me on the very morning that I was engaged in writing this section.

> I used The Miracle Midget to read the whole of chapters one and two from Ephesians to two thousand people gathered at the Central Methodist Hall in London last year. It took me two

minutes to locate The Midget, and another three to extract the magnifying glass from the torn lining of my jacket, where I had placed it before coming on to the platform. I stopped three times to apologize for stumbling over words, and received the only standing ovation of the evening after completing my reading. Now The Midget goes everywhere with me. Thanks for all you do.

–James Jonas, Liverpool

The Shining Visage

A recent development, our Shining Visage Bible reflects the fact that we are determined not to be left behind in an age of advanced technology. The SV, as we call it, is ideal for the Churchman or woman who has worked hard to establish an aura of mysticism and other-worldliness and is now wanting to take the public projection of these qualities to another, slightly higher, level.

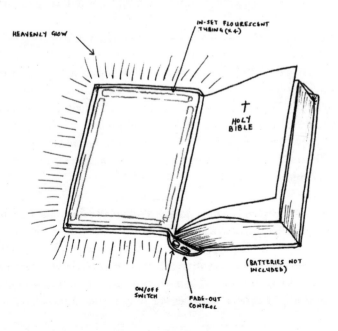

Quite simply, the Shining Visage *(forty pounds per unit, including postage and packing, two AA batteries required, not included in price — see illustration)* is a large, hard-backed Bible, normal in every way except that an almost microscopically thin lighting tube has been set into the top, bottom and sides of the inside cover. A button concealed beneath the spine allows the user to operate the illumination effect without any apparent movement of his or her hands. An additional *fading* feature avoids the danger of a less than mystical, abrupt descent into darkness.

Researchers here at Headquarters and in the field have commented on the wisdom of ensuring that the lighting involved is low-powered to the point of near invisibility. Much of the value of the SV is dependent upon observers finding it difficult to trust what they have seen with their own eyes.

> On Tuesday night, did Daniel Feltham (one of our earliest customers for the SV) really have a heavenly light shining all around his face as he read from the Bible, or did we dream it?

This is the type of question that the Shining Visage is designed to provoke. We would, incidentally, recommend that users of the SV should be experienced practitioners who have learned the value of strict economy in the use of a facility like this. Our aim is not to create the impression of an old-fashioned magic lantern show. It would be more than regrettable if the practice of Churchmanship were to acquire an air of Monty Pythonesque absurdity.

Testimonials have been satisfyingly positive. Here is one striking and informative example.

> I first used The Shining Visage Bible in the last of a series of inter-church Lenten Bible-study groups. Looking up during the time of candlelit prayer at the end of the meeting, I noticed that the only other person with her eyes open was a slightly stern lady named Jane Caxton. Her main contribution to the fortnightly meetings had been an assertion that, in this age, Christianity

was a no-nonsense business in which the miraculous did not occur and was not needed. Switching on my SV lights with only the gentlest pressure of my right forefinger, I gazed into my open Bible and allowed slightly less than a minute before switching them off. At the end of the meeting I noticed Jane Caxton drawing people around her and whispering something with great animation, indicating me with her hand once or twice as she spoke. I left almost immediately, of course, waving farewell to the group from the door with a small, angelic smile of unconscious spirituality on my face.

Since that evening my church experience has been revolutionized. *Everyone* wants to hear my opinion on just about *everything.* Thank you, Churchmanship Headquarters, for the wonderful Shining Visage Bible. It has changed my life. Jane Caxton is pursuing the possibility of joining an order.

P.S. Do remind your members to carry extra AA batteries with them, as the divine aura does cut out rather suddenly with a high-pitched buzzing noise when they expire.

–Doon Appleton, Carlisle

The Crafty Concordance Bible

The use of a concordance is not in itself a Churchmanship ploy, although many of us have experienced the way in which preachers and teachers employ this useful tool with a slick facility that would make Churchmen and women proud. Now we are pleased to announce that we have made it possible for our members to amaze all those present with a complex knowledge of the Bible that involves no *apparent* use of a concordance.

The Crafty Concordance Bible, our brand-new product (*reserve your copy now for our special pre-publication discounted price of just fifty-three pounds per volume, including everlasting batteries and postage and packing – see illustration*) is on the face of it a perfectly normal, if somewhat bulky, version of the Scriptures. Inside, however, the text is printed around a square, hollowed-out space that allows the insertion of a small but highly efficient electronic concordance with high-clarity screen. This allows the user to whisk from reference to reference with bewildering speed and accuracy, thus astonishing other members of the group or congregation.

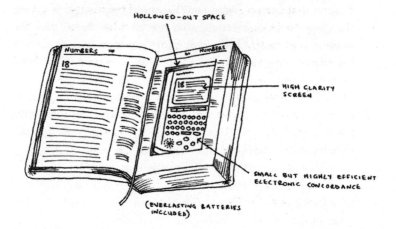

This essential piece of church equipment is not yet available for sale, but here is just one of the encouraging reports from our field testers.

I used The Crafty Concordance Bible at a small gathering in my local church where we were discussing the issue of 'sacrifice' in the Bible. Having surreptitiously typed in the relevant word, I found that the CCB offered me a list of more than one hundred and seventy instances of its use, complete with references. Frankly, from thereon I was magnificent. To say that the other members of the group were impressed would be an understatement, but let me also issue a warning that might usefully be included in the instructions that will eventually be issued with this product.

Towards the end of the meeting I was so distracted by positive comments from person A to my left that I failed to register person B crossing from the other side of the room to compare a verse in his Bible with the same verse in my version (*see diagram*). So close did he come to detecting the electronic concordance that I was forced to slam my Bible shut with disproportionate violence and appear to take deep offence at the fact that person A had complimented me instead of giving the glory to God. Her husband, a man who throughout the evening had clearly been finding my expertise with Scripture extremely irksome, then asked me how I would feel about eating my own Bible with the Pentateuch as a starter, Joshua to Malachi as main course, the Gospels as dessert, Acts to Jude as an assorted cheese platter and Revelation as a small coffee with mints. I replied, with godly dignity, that I would pray for him. Chaos ensued, and I left.

A wonderful product, but to be used with care.

−Carlton Summers, Milton Mowbray

Modern Bible Versions

As well as staying abreast of technological advances with regard to Scripture, we at Churchmanship Headquarters are more than happy to acknowledge and benefit from recent efforts to make the Bible more accessible and relevant to those who would not normally read it. In particular we applaud the dumbing down process by which the body of Scripture is being gradually reduced to an attractively pale version of its former self. Interestingly, Letitia Parsons of Crewe has suggested (and here Letitia may be just a tad premature) that the Bible of the future will be entitled 'The Two-Sentence Bible', its entire contents and accompanying concordance appearing in this form:

THE TWO-SENTENCE BIBLE

Old Testament
1:1   God made the world and it was all right, but then it got messed up by people.

New Testament
1:1   Jesus came and made it all right again.

Concordance

AGAIN
NT   1:1   it all right **a.**

ALL
OT   1:1   it was **a.** right
NT   1:1   made it **a.** right

AND
OT   1:1   the world **a.** it was
NT   1:1   came **a.** made it

BUT
OT   1:1   was all right, **b.** then

BY

OT   1:1 messed up **b.** people

CAME

NT   1:1 Jesus **c.** and made

GOD

OT   1:1 **g.** made the world

GOT

OT   1:1 then it **g.** messed

IT

OT   1:1 and **i.** was all

OT   1:1 then **i.** got messed

NT   1:1 and made **i.** all right

JESUS

NT   1:1 **j.** came and made

MADE

OT   1:1 God **m.** the world

NT   1:1 came and **m.** it all right

MESSED

OT   1:1 got **m.** up by

PEOPLE

OT   1:1 got messed up by **p.**

RIGHT

OT   1:1 was all **r.**, but

NT   1:1 it all **r.** again

THE

OT   1:1 made **t.** world and

THEN

OT   1:1 but **t.** it got messed

UP

OT   1:1 got messed **u.** by

WAS

OT   1:1 and it **w.** all

WORLD

OT   1:1 made the **w.** and

Letitia's vision of such a cataclysmically uncluttered Bible may be a viable project for development in the future, but in the meantime we have been experimenting here at Churchmanship Headquarters with a version of Scripture that employs teenage speak. Here, for instance, is the 'nang' version of Moses' encounter with God at the burning bush.

And Moses like saw this like burning bush and he like app-roached it.

And God was like Mo-o-o-o-ose-man! This is like Go-o-o-o-od!

And Moses was like wow! Awesome! This is nang! Heh, G-dog, you are a ledge!

And God was like talk to the bush 'cause the face ain't listenin'. And get your shoes off, man. You are on like holy ground.

And Moses was like come on you re-eds!

And God was like no not that kind of holy ground. Not like Old Trafford. It's like holy because I'm here and I'm like Go-o-o-o-od.

And Moses was like oh, my Go-o-od! Oh, my Go-o-o-o-od!!

And God was like where you heading, Mose-man?

And Moses was like you know, find some mates, sink a few ales, talk about girls, cotch down for the night. You know the scene, G-dog.

And God was like no I do not know the scene, and stop calling me G-dog, Mose-man, or I shall like smite you.

And Moses was like a-a-a-a-a-a-a-h!

And God was like thing is Mose-man the like Israelites are having such a phat-free time in Egypt.

And Moses was like oh, I *so* totally get what you're saying.

And God was like well someone has got to like lead them out to the Promised Land, man, where it will all like flow with milk and honey.

And Moses was like euch! Milk and honey sounds a bit gloopy and sticky dude. Couldn't it be like lager and Hobnobs.

And God was like no it can't Mose-man. You cannot make hob-nobs like flow. Anyway, I'm like Go-o-o-o-od so I decide. I'll like sort out the refreshments and someone else can, you know, threaten Pharaoh.

And Moses was like heh, threaten Pharaoh! That is e-e-e-pic! That is i-i-i-i-ideal! That is – Ah! Can I just say, G-dog, that I am *so* not the man for that Pharaoh threatening job?

And God was like well, you are, and it is you, Mose-man. You are the man!

And Moses was like shud-u-u-up! Heh, no way, G-dog, dude, I'm already a mouldy. Uber vanilla. Clappin', man. Know what I mean? Anyway I'm like no good at the nang.

And God was like okay, wuss, you can take your tin-grin klingon Aaron to like hold your hand.

And Moses was like gratz, G-dog! I'll take the gig.

And when Moses had like found his shoes at last and gone God was like oh, my Go-o-o-od! What a loser! Why didn't I smite the zep when I had the chance?

Opinions are at present divided about the advisability of releasing passages of this kind for general use. While there is clearly a great deal to be gained by the trivialization of Scripture, we must never lose sight of the danger that readers might end up having 'fun'. As a general rule it would be wise to regard the words 'Bible' and 'fun' as being mutually exclusive, except of course when it is strategically desirable to provide a counter to serious exegetical study. In this case an interruption of the kind quoted below can be very helpful.

'Don't think I don't appreciate the seriousness and dignity of Scripture, but I would just like to ask if the folks here agree with me when I say that our God is a God who wants to laugh and have fun with his people. What does everyone think? Shut me up if I'm being silly or speaking out of turn . . .'

Bible Discussionmanship

Conscientious Churchmen and women will never allow ignorance of Scripture to prevent them from holding their own in discussions that involve the Bible. Methods vary, but it is well to remember that simple ploys can often be the best. My Uncle Dexter Caplin, for instance, used the same technique over and over again in a wide variety of situations, simply dropping his two sentences more or less at random into the centre of the discussion.

'I think we're back to Zephaniah with this one. Does anyone else go along with me on that?'

Uncle Dexter had never read Zephaniah, of course, but then hardly anyone else had either, so redirectional success was virtually guaranteed. Everyone would feel obliged to knit their brows and poke around in the book of Zephaniah trying to work out why Uncle Dexter felt they should be 'back to it'. A fine ploy.

It was Uncle Dexter who also taught me the correct procedure at those awkward moments when someone else proves you wrong by quoting Scripture.

'The most important thing,' he explained, 'is to avoid any display of panic. As soon as your opponent has made his point, pick up your own Bible and start leafing through energetically and purposefully as though you know exactly what you're looking for. Finally, let out a little sigh of satisfaction as you appear to locate the verses you were trying to find. Settle the book on your knee, tap some random portion of the text briskly with your finger, raise that same finger in a confident, lecturing manner, and say:

' "Okay, Jeff, I absolutely hear what you're saying with that last quote, but with all due respect, old friend, you just haven't taken account of – "

'Break off abruptly at this point as if the better side of yourself has suddenly come to the fore, slap your Bible shut with an engagingly rueful little smile, and say:

' "No, I won't do it. I simply won't do it. Others may think there's some profit in these juvenile Scripture duels, but I don't, and nor do you, Jeff, I'm quite sure. There's more to life and faith than being right. I'd prefer to accept that I'm wrong and continue in fellowship with another believer. Jeff, my dear brother, let's agree to differ and leave it at that."

'Nine times out of ten that will be the end of the matter. The "duel" is postponed, and you, the Churchman, are revealed as a man of faith and charity who could have "won" but preferred to respect the dignity of Scripture and ensure peace than to score points by merely "being right". An excellent outcome.'

—————— NEW TECHNOLOGICAL ——————
ADVANCES

In addition to technological advances in the area of Bible production we are pleased to announce two other highly innovative devices for the consideration of students and members.

(1) Automated Arm Raiser

This cunning device, developed here in our own workshop for those who find the physical side of worship wearying or tedious, enables active participation in worship without *any effort whatsoever* – even when the Churchman or woman concerned is enjoying a light *sleep.* The Automated Arm Raiser (*available from Churchmanship Headquarters, price sixty-three pounds per unit including battery charger and postage and packing – see illustration*) consists of a very light, plastic-coated metal framework worn under the coat or jacket. This in turn is connected to two similarly coated, hinged arms fitting discreetly inside the sleeves of the wearer. Both arms culminate in soft rubber pads that nestle into the palms of the hands, thus avoiding unpleasant chafing or soreness.

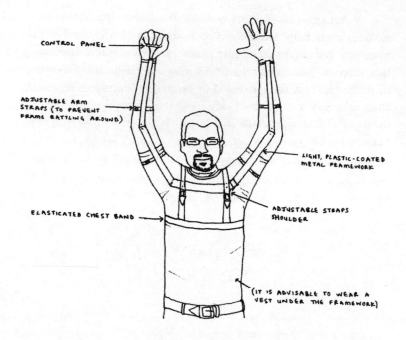

CONTROL PANEL

ADJUSTABLE ARM
STRAPS (TO PREVENT
FRAME RATTLING AROUND)

LIGHT, PLASTIC-COATED
METAL FRAMEWORK

ELASTICATED CHEST BAND

ADJUSTABLE STRAPS
SHOULDER

(IT IS ADVISABLE TO WEAR A
VEST UNDER THE FRAMEWORK)

A simple control panel set into one of these pads allows the worshipper to easily control the Automated Arm Raiser by the discreet use of an index finger (*see illustration*).

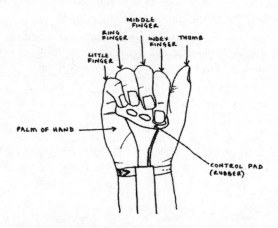

MIDDLE
FINGER

RING
FINGER

INDEX
FINGER

THUMB

LITTLE
FINGER

PALM OF HAND

CONTROL PAD
(RUBBER)

A second control panel set into the metal framework itself makes it possible for the wearer, using his other hand, to pre-set the device so that his arms are raised and lowered at intervals of one, two, three or four minutes, according to taste. This amazing piece of technology makes it possible for the user to drop his head to his chest and have a refreshing little sleep during worship, confident in the knowledge that the Automated Arm Raiser will, as it were, do the praising for him (*see illustration*).

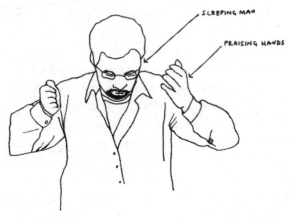

Reports from our field testers have been uniformly positive, other than the one we publish here which has prompted us to iron out the slight technical problem described.

I wore the Automated Arm Raiser to a meeting of our local Assemblies of God church and switched it on at a pre-set level as the worship leader launched into the first chorus of the morning. Unfortunately, some gremlin must have crept into the mechanism. Instead of raising my arms slowly to the vertical and holding them there for two minutes before allowing them to gently descend, it went completely out of control and began to raise and lower my arms over and over again at a ludicrously frantic rate. Panic-stricken, I called out several times, 'Oh, God, I don't how to stop it!'

Fortunately, people in the same row must have assumed that I was manifesting some new wave or movement of the Spirit, and within minutes half the congregation were flapping their arms wildly up and down in time with mine, and crying out in unison, 'Oh, God, I don't know how to stop it!'

The next phase of malfunction was, if anything, even more bizarre. Instead of raising my arms in parallel with each other, the machine began to operate left and right arms alternately so that I appeared to be executing a stiff and insanely rapid walking motion with the top half of my body. Eventually I had the presence of mind to remember to move the switch to 'off' on my palm pad and the nightmare was ended.

One positive aspect of all this was that when I returned to the church a few weeks later I discovered that the two varieties of arm movement had been incorporated into the confessional section of the service. Furthermore, two people were electing to walk round and round the edge of the church, shouting as they went about not being able to stop it. Their rigid, alternate arm movements made them look like berserk versions of Spotty Dog, a character who older people may remember from the children's television programme *The Woodentops* many years ago.

Despite this satisfying outcome, and much as I enjoyed being hailed as one of a new wave of Devonshire Prophets on my return, I would most earnestly suggest that you solve these little mechanical problems before making the product available for purchase.

–Desmond Moore, Torquay

As you can imagine, we were most intrigued by the way in which Desmond Moore accidentally discovered such a fascinating ploy, but he may rest assured that we have located the cause of the fault. The Automated Arm Raiser is now perfected and ready for use.

(2) The Armpit Angel Voice Sound System

This sophisticated piece of equipment comprises a music system hooked to the belt, with wires running beneath the clothes to two tiny but adequately powered speakers affixed by a Velcro-style attachment to the hairs of both underarms (*see illustration*). At an appropriate moment in any church activity the Churchman is able to switch on the device and allow the very faint but unmistakeable sound of angelic voices raised in song to emanate from his armpits. Of course, as the user raises his arms, the volume will increase, and vice versa. A very nice touch.

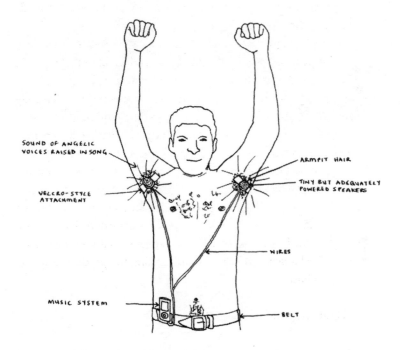

Unfortunately, the Armpit Angel Voice Sound System is not yet ready for general use, as one or two minor problems remain unsolved. For example, brisk removal of the loudspeakers from the armpits of our testing operatives is still causing them to go screaming round the lab, and there are intermittent instances of the device transmitting distorted Radio 4 programmes and irritable messages to mobile pizza delivery operatives instead of angelic voices. In a church setting the latter phenomenon in particular would be bizarre, if not grotesque. Work continues, so watch this space!

Section 10
LOOKING GOODMANSHIP

As a Churchman or woman in good standing you will know the supreme importance of looking good in any and every situation.

————FAMOUS PERSONMANSHIP————

For the dedicated Churchman and woman, irony was ever a thing of delight. Consider, for example, that period from the nineteen-sixties through to the mid-nineteen-nineties when hugely popular figures at such events as Greenbelt and Spring Harvest could regularly be heard decrying the personality cult that had developed – not just among young people, but throughout the modern church. Sadly, in recent years this irony has been largely ironed out, as it were, but there remains a general appetite for contact with famous people that can and should be exploited by those of us who see opportunities to do so. Let us learn from the masters.

Stottmanship
Darley Jameson, using a sub-ploy that he described as Stottmanship, always kept a supply of books, some in his guest bedroom and some in his sitting room, that had apparently been personally signed by the authors. A copy of *Understanding the Bible*, for instance, published by John R.W. Stott in 2003, was inscribed on the title page with this handwritten message:

> *To Darley, my mentor and friend, with grateful thanks yet again for your patient and untiring assistance. This book is really half yours.*
>
> *All my love, Stotty*

In a copy of *Basic Christianity*, a volume published seven years earlier in 1996, Stott appeared to have written these words:

> *My very best to you, Darley, in appreciation of all those long afternoons and evenings that we spent putting this stuff together. What a privilege it was to sit at your feet. I shall always be thankful for your generosity and humility. My name is on the front cover, but your mind and heart are on every page.*
>
> *Ever yours, Stotty*

Jameson was never less than thorough. Having discovered that a fellow-Churchman owned a letter genuinely written by John Stott, he borrowed it and spent hours painstakingly practising the hand-writing until his copies were virtually indistinguishable from the original script. Nor was he crude in the methods he adopted for bringing these books to the attention of his visitors.

'Sleep well,' he would say mildly to a guest as he handed him a glass of malted milk which had in just about every case already been politely refused by guests who had no idea what it was, 'I think there are a couple of books up there if you need something to get you off. Help yourself, old chap.'

If the guest appeared for breakfast the next morning waving *Basic Christianity* and commenting excitedly on the inscription, Jameson would knit his brows, look vague and slightly puzzled for a moment, then say something like, 'Oh, good gracious, you mean old Stotty. Yes, that's right, I'd forgotten. We did do quite a lot of stuff together at one time. Fancy that book still being around. I was wondering where it had got to.'

It would have mattered very little which book the guest had selected, either in his bedroom or downstairs in the lounge. Judging by what was written on the title pages of more than half the items in Jameson's library, he had exerted huge influence on just about every significant Christian writer of the past forty years or more. Without Jameson's advice and support Henri Nouwen would never have properly understood the parable of the prodigal son, Philip Yancey might have been significantly less amazed by grace, Rick Warren would have been sadly lacking in the purpose required to drive his church and John Ortberg would still be wondering whether to get out of the boat or not. There were exceptions, of course. Books by such writers as Adrian Plass and Jeff Lucas bore no such inscriptions. Jameson hadn't bothered. Very understandable. The aim of the Churchman is, after all, to impress.

Proactive Famous Personmanship
By contrast, Damian Eccles of Southport advocates a much more proactive, muscular approach to the execution of Famous Personmanship, as exemplified by the strikingly successful ploy he devised for the purpose of striking up acquaintanceship with the Archbishop of Canterbury when that dignitary visited St Botolph's the Lesser in Wolverhampton in the autumn of 2004.

Eccles appeared (unapologetically late) at the church hall buffet reception dressed in trainers, jeans and tee-shirt with his hair flopped sulkily over his eyes and a thick file clutched under one arm. He gave the appearance of being distracted and impatient, as though this was the last place on earth he needed or wanted to be when practical, constructive activities connected with the real needs of real people awaited his attention elsewhere.

For the first twenty minutes of the reception he leaned listlessly against the wall at the side of the hall, greeting a handful of the least important-looking people with considerable warmth,[25] but pointedly ignoring the Archbishop, who was trying to sip tea and eat finger food as he played flame to a swirling cloud of adoring moths.

Eventually, with a little yawn, Eccles levered his weight off the wall and slouched moodily through the crowds and across the room, apparently unaware of the fact that he was approaching the

---

[25] Keen students will quickly make the connection between this element of Damian Eccles' ploy and the strategy of David Trump in embracing the least attractive women in his church at the Exchanging of the Peace (*see section on Communion Ploys, above*).

guest of honour. It was as he passed the tall, robed figure that Eccles suddenly thrust his file into the startled Archbishop's arms and leaped almost full-length to rescue a perfectly securely held dish piled with sandwiches from the hands of a perfectly competent, deeply alarmed serving girl.

Recovering himself modestly from his heroics, Damian Eccles seemed to realize with a start that his file, labelled in very large capital letters 'LIVING AND WORKING WITH DRUG-ADDICTED SINGLE TEENAGE MOTHERS IN DEPRIVED INNER-CITY ESTATES – A NEW PROJECT' (*similar, specially prepared folders with a choice of cover legends available from Churchmanship Headquarters, twelve pounds per folder including postage and packing – see illustration*[26]), had been dumped on the Archbishop of Canterbury. As he said to me on the telephone a few days later, his ploy turned out to be good for at least fifteen minutes of conversation, after which the Archbishop had insisted on staying in touch to hear how the 'new project' worked out.

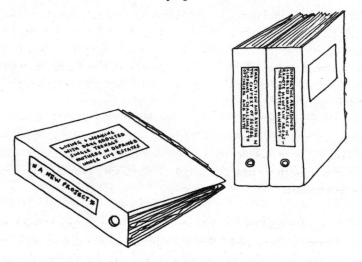

---

[26] Other available file titles include:
Supporting abandoned limbless amnesiacs in remote mountain areas – the forgotten minority
Emaciation and autism in the context of severe flooding – challenges to optimism and faith
Outreach and assistance to those crushed by falling walls and ceilings – putting the beam back on their faces.

I need hardly add that there was no such project. As Damian himself expressed it, if a committee were to be assembled with the express purpose of defining the one thing that D. Eccles would least like to do in the whole world, it would probably conclude that living and working with drug-addicted, single teenage mothers in a deprived inner city estate was very near the top of the list, if not on the absolute pinnacle.

On the other hand, the successful ploy made it possible for Damian to refer with casual ease to things that were said when 'me and the Arch had a chat'. People were most impressed. A highly successful ploy.

SINCERITY AND CHURCHMANSHIP

Perhaps the least justified criticism of Churchmanship theory and practice is the suggestion that our organization has no investment in sincerity. Our reply to this calumny is very simple. Sincerity is an essential aspect of church living for the Churchman, and we at Headquarters are anxious to assist our students in developing this very valuable talent for themselves. Having made this important point, it is undoubtedly the case that, in this area, individual ploys are suited to individual Churchmen and women. For this reason we have decided to publish a selection of extracts from letters sent by those who are happy to offer their personal solutions for general use.

'I have found that a light coating of Preparation H rubbed in gently above and below the eyes imparts a smooth rigidity to the skin. This facilitates a contextual steadiness of gaze that is as sincere as anything else I have ever seen or managed for myself.'

–Georg Shrub, Washington

'I have discovered two workable solutions to the sincerity problem. Both involve the use of considerable mental energy during my talks. In the first I simply imagine that I am married to either the late Bernard Manning, or the not-late-enough Max Clifford. Intensive contemplation of either of these scenarios casts a shadow of such sadness and despair over my features that every word I say is greeted with rapt attention.

My second solution is to tell myself that I have just sixty seconds and one chance to spell the word *diarrhoea* correctly, otherwise I shall be flayed alive and fed to ravenous pigs. The intense, concentrated panic generated by this inner process produces a facial expression that could hardly be more genuine.'

–Iris Kawl, Canterbury

'I wrestled with my own failure over sincerity issues for a long time. Indeed, there was a point where I came very close to losing faith altogether in Churchmanship principles. Fortunately, I recently encountered an amazing man called Butterfield[27] who has years of experience in this field. His advice has made all the difference. At his suggestion I now take a pin or a needle with me when I speak to groups of people. At a point when I am particularly keen to show that I passionately believe what I am saying, I secretly stick the pin into the fleshy part of my upper leg. If I stick it in hard enough, an involuntary gasp or sob of pain breaks into the very words I am saying. For instance, the reading of this verse from Revelation chapter three was hugely successful:

---

[27] We are, of course, well acquainted with Butterfield, as sections of this report indicate. Indeed, we adopted his Pin or Needle Ploy as part of our formal training course as long ago as 1983. Specially designed, long-life needles threaded on lengths of invisible fishing line and fastened to handy clip-on belt attachments (*three pounds fifty including postage and packing – see illustration*) have been available as standard issue since that date.

Behold I stand at the door and knock. If anyone – *aaaah!* – hears my voice and opens the door . . . etc.

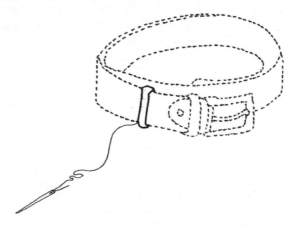

Obviously the ploy should not be used more than twice in any one talk or presentation, but I have to say that the effect on listeners is spectacular. Thank you, Butterfield. You have restored my faith.'

–Sebastian Rook, Wantage

'My way of tackling the sincerity thing when I preach is to take a crime novel or something I'm really enjoying up to the platform with me without anyone seeing. I hide it under my Bible on the lectern, and when I get to the bit of my talk where I want to look deeply moved I slide the novel out from under the Bible and read a page or two. I probably stay completely still because I'm really enjoying getting on with my book and totally absorbed, but from where the punters[28] are it looks as

---

[28] Although we applaud Mark Williams' ingenuity and willingness to share his ploy with fellow students, we would like to dissociate ourselves from the practice of referring to church people as 'punters'. Becoming a Churchman must never mean that respect and courtesy go out of the window. After all, they are valuable assets.

though I'm so stirred up by what I'm saying that I've had to concentrate for half a minute to conquer my emotions and pull myself together. One time I read a chapter and a half before suddenly remembering where I was. Afterwards someone said it was the best talk they'd ever heard!

Stops you getting bored as well.'

—Mark Williams, Cardiff

'My sincerity ploy is basically to imagine that I am about to eat a bowl of cold tripe soaked in rancid olive oil. Care must be taken, though. The white face and staring eyes are very effective, but there have been times when I came within an ace of vomiting over the front row.'

—Gloria Marsh, Broom

Section 11

DISCONCERTMANSHIP

There is undoubtedly a sense in which the ongoing task of the Churchman or woman who truly wishes to make a difference is always to *disconcert*. As the great Durham Steadman so rightly and succinctly remarks:

> 'There is no point in putting putting someone off off until tomorrow if you can put them off today.'

Nevertheless, we have included a specific section on this subject because some of the ploys involved are so simple, and so narrowly and exquisitely contained within the term. Generally, the one to whom the ploy is directed will be termed the *disconcertee*.

─────── GOOD WISHMANSHIP ───────

Like many of the very best ploys, Good Wishmanship is deceptively simple in its essentials but cannot be operated without the skill and concentration that is only to be found in the practised Churchman or woman.

When I was working in a large Methodist church in Manchester as general administrator (a task that I had been told to make my own and, through massive delegation, had managed to turn into a job that required minimal attendance and absolutely no work whatsoever on my part by the time I had been there for three months), a man named Norman Colsworthy was interviewed for the nerve-jinglingly-entitled post of Music Minister. Colsworthy was ominously grown-up and promising on the day of his visit, so I thought it best to bring Good Wishmanship into play just before he was due to meet the choir and musicians of the church.

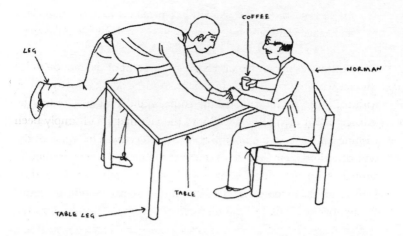

Finding him nervously finishing a cup of coffee in the church canteen, I wasted no time. Keen to convey the tension and urgency of the moment, I balanced unsteadily (and unnecessarily) on one leg (*see illustration*) and leaned across the longest side of the table at which he was sitting. Wrapping one of his hands in both of mine I looked deeply into his eyes and spoke with hushed intensity.

MYSELF: Norman, I just – you don't mind if I call you Norman, do you?

COLSWORTHY: Er, no, no, of course not. What er . . . ?

MYSELF: Norman, I know you're just about to go and meet all the music people, but – (*trebling the intensity*) listen, mate, I've just had a phone call (*this was true, my mother had phoned to ask me to come round and put the wheely-bins out for her later in the evening*) and we just want you to know that you're in all our thoughts and prayers at this very difficult time. We want you to be aware of that, we really do.

COLSWORTHY: Well, thanks, but . . . I don't quite understand. Do you mean you've heard something about – ?

MYSELF: (*squeezing his hand even more tightly, then placing one finger against my lips as though suggesting it would be better to postpone the revelation of some great sorrow)* Hush, Norman – go to the musicians and I shall wait for you here. Go now. Go to them. Go quickly . . .

Colsworthy was perspiring and edgy to the point of distraction in his contact with the choir and musicians. And he was distinctly tetchy with me when he returned to the canteen and I made sure that he learned about my mother's call and the fact that I had simply been wishing him well in the next part of his interview. This was not the type of attitude our church was looking for at all, as we unanimously agreed. A much more suitable candidate emerged soon after that. Less musical but more easily played, as it were. A crucial point. Remember that, from the point of view of the Churchman, the person who is given the task of organizing the choir and musicians must be *run by them* and not the other way round.

——AM I THE ONLY ONEMANSHIP——

Designed and developed by Gillian Jessop of Streatham, this well-conceived distracting ploy is designed to interfere with a workshop or seminar that is going well and needs to be creatively disrupted. At a point where real progress is being made the Churchman will ask (preferably in a manner that suggests he knows full well he will not be given a hearing) if he is going to be allowed to say something. On being granted permission he will speak with a carefully judged tone of amiable exasperation, together with a slight but rapid shaking movement of the head.

'I'd just like to ask this. Am I the only one who really hasn't got the faintest idea what's going on here, or how all this stuff is supposed to help us?'

Group leaders who are inexperienced, or genuinely caring but nervous, are extremely vulnerable to this clever ploy. Always be aware, however, that Churchmen and women can crop up anywhere, and by their very nature are difficult to detect.

Miles Thatcham, an old student of mine and a very able Churchman, once used Gillian's ploy without realizing that the man in charge of the seminar on Practical Spirituality, Jeremy Crown-Carstairs (*see section on The Art of Avoiding Choruses with Actions, above*), was a Churchman of enormous ability. Crown-Carstairs' counter-ploy to Thatcham's question was all that one would expect from such an accomplished practitioner.

'Wow! I want to take that question and run with it,' he replied, jumping to his feet with huge enthusiasm and energy. 'Everyone vote now. Come on! Put your hands up if you agree with Miles that I'm wasting your time. I'll be more than happy to accept it as the Lord's guidance if that is the case. And I want to sincerely thank you, Miles, for the courage and commitment you've shown in speaking from the heart. Not everybody would have been able to do that. You're a star, mate.'

He smiled around at everybody, and, my goodness, I have to say that Crown-Carstairs was better at allowing his face to light up with radiant good humour than any other Churchman I have known. This is especially impressive when you consider that he was and is a snappy, disagreeable type of man who finds most people intensely annoying and doesn't really *like* anybody.

Of course, not a single hand was raised, and Thatcham was shunned and glared at by the rest of the group for the remainder of the session. We all have to learn, and it is as well to learn from an expert.

——— HELPFUL TRACTMANSHIP ———

In these days of desktop publishing there are so many new opportunities for the enterprising Churchman or woman. Here at Headquarters we have been engaged in the production of a selection of leaflet-like tracts, their titles printed in large fluorescent block capitals (*available from Churchmanship Headquarters, price four pounds fifty pence per tract, including postage and packing – see illustration*).

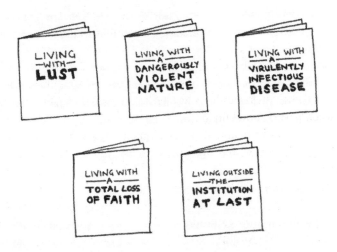

Titles published so far include:

Living with Lust (purple lettering)

Living with a Dangerously Violent Nature (red lettering)

Living with a Virulently Infectious Disease (bright green lettering with very small khaki spots)

Living with Total Loss of Faith (black lettering)

Living Outside the Institution at Last (neon orange lettering)

Any Churchman or woman can enjoy success with these powerfully vivid little presentations by following six easy-to-understand steps.

(1) Select a moment when you know that the potential disconcertee is sitting in a room with other people, possibly engaged in a meeting of some kind.

(2) Blunder in through the door without knocking.

(3) Appear to not notice the others in the room and go straight to the person concerned, holding out a copy of, for instance, Living with Lust as you approach him.

(4) Use the following form of words: 'Oh, Roger, I've got a copy of that booklet you said you wanted to have a look – '

(5) Suddenly glance around in horror and say, 'Oh, sorry! I got the time wrong. I didn't realize you were in the middle of . . . Sorry! I really am so very sorry . . .'

(6) Suddenly realize that the vivid purple words on the cover of the tract are visible to all those present, the more so because you have been slowly revolving as you apologize. Make a bad job of concealing them as you back out through the door looking mortified with embarrassment. Do not hang about. Trust your ploy. Bear in mind that there is nothing the disconcertee can do or say after you have left that will *not* make things ten times worse for him than they already are.

It is important to emphasize that the right form of words *must* be used in the execution of this ploy. Samuel Kettering, now of Sandborne, recounts a distressing experience at a United Reform Church just outside Whitstable. Kettering rushed into a meeting room where a man called Alvin Sampson was about to lead a brainstorming session on ways to increase the faith of church members. What Kettering failed to realize was that Alvin Sampson was, and is, one of those rare geniuses that emerge from the Churchmanship stable. I should add that he is a man whose privately expressed statement of faith is 'I suppose there might be something out there. A sort of force – who knows? I certainly don't.'

Kettering adhered to the first three stages of the ploy perfectly, waving the Living with Total Loss of Faith tract for all to see as he entered. It was in the execution of step four that his mistake was made, and this short but vivid piece of dialogue ensued.

KETTERING: Oh, Alvin, I've brought that booklet along for you.
SAMPSON: (*completely calm and without batting an eyelid*) Oh, cheers for bringing it back, Sammy. Did it touch the spot for you? That's what I've been praying for, my old chum. Thanks for getting it to me in time for all the friends here to have a look-see. That's what I got it for. I've seen it help so many people. Tell you what, I'm a bit busy at the moment, but I'll see you later

to get some feedback – we'll spend some special time. Promise! (*winking conspiratorially and wagging a finger with affectionate, mock severity*) And don't you go giving up, or anything silly like that, will you, my man?

Kettering, newly branded as a needy disciple of Sampson's with no faith and a need for 'special time', backed miserably out of the room, unable to think of anything else to say, leaving Sampson to shake his head significantly and point out in troubled, responsible tones that this was exactly the kind of problem they were gathering to discuss.

People sometimes say 'Sticks and stones may break my bones, but words can never hurt me.' This statement, almost certainly written by a Churchman or woman, is clearly not true, but remember – you do have to get the words *right.*

──────── GRACEMANSHIP ────────

Alvin Sampson, well known for his brilliant counter-ploy in Helpful Tractmanship and other strokes of Disconcertmanship genius, developed this ploy as a means of thoroughly disconcerting groups of dinner guests that he had invited to his own home. Sampson would bring the meal to the table with friendly, bluff enthusiasm, then, after serving everyone but himself with all that they needed he would jovially cry, 'Don't you dare wait for me, you hungry old load of gannets. Tuck in while it's good and hot.'

As soon as most of the guests had at least one forkful of food in their mouths he would fold his hands, bow his head and say in a quiet, almost apologetic, voice, 'I always like to say a little grace before I start my meal.'

Sampson reports that the gentle clatter of knives and forks being lowered to plates, and the soft rustle of serviettes being applied to the corners of mouths as embarrassed guests hurriedly curtail their eating activities, is music to his ears.

————ASK TROUBLING QUESTIONS————

It is always a good policy to unsettle both individuals and groups with questions that are difficult or impossible to answer, not least because Christians notoriously tend to be perched on the very precipice of guilt and confusion. The use of this ploy is, in any case, an established means of control in most branches of the church, and it is by no means utilized exclusively by Churchmen and women. However, during my time at Great Malvern I had the opportunity to develop and refine some of these questions, including my personal favourite, the *1 John Jangle*.

This is particularly useful with enthusiastic young people, however field reports suggest that any person in whom zeal and lack of confidence are combined will be affected similarly, regardless of their age. Procedure is not difficult, but perfect timing will make all the difference.

Let us say, for instance, that your potential disconcertee is one of those young men in his mid-twenties who is an important part of the worship band,[29] and is also responsible for controlling all the sound equipment used in your church. These young men (usually called Phil[30]) are generally very busy indeed on service days – checking

---

[29] In mentioning the worship band I am reminded of a ploy created by Violet Banning of Wigton in Cumbria. For strategic reasons of her own Violet was quite often involved in leading the service in a large ex-Brethren church at the edge of town on the side nearest to Penrith. The worship band consisted of two singers, a pianist, a saxophonist, a violinist and two guitarists. For four Sundays in a row Violet made a point of saying exactly the same thing after the minister had finished his talk.

'Now it's time for our last chorus, so would the musicians and the guitarists please come and take their places again?'

On the fifth occasion that she extended this invitation, one of the guitarists began to shout angrily from the body of the church and, in the end, had to be physically restrained and removed. I am told that the quality of Violet's innocent bewilderment was quite remarkable.

[30] Or possibly Pete.

equipment, testing microphones, tuning instruments and setting up visuals. Post yourself in a strategic spot, leaning on the side of the mixing desk perhaps, and at a moment when Phil is totally focussed on the job in hand, fix him with a solemnly prophetic eye (*see illustration*) and say these words in a calm but penetrating tone.

'Phil, how can you be sure that you know Jesus Christ?'

PHIL/PETE

If your timing and delivery hit the mark, Phil will be completely thrown off balance by this simple question. Distracted from the obvious truth that his immediate responsibilities to God lie in the practical tasks of the moment, he will flail around helplessly in the hope of hitting upon the right answer to the question. Ignore all these stumbling attempts. Merely say quietly as you turn to walk away:

'Read the second chapter of the first letter of John, Phil.'

Fastidious Churchmen and women might choose to read this passage for themselves, but there is not a lot of point in doing so. The main purpose of the ploy will almost certainly have been achieved. Disturbed by his inability to answer such a simple question, Phil is likely to develop a twitch on his sliders that will adversely affect everything from the introduction to the final prayer.

Phil's flailing response to a simple question is precisely what we are endeavouring to provoke with all of our Troubling Questions. Satisfyingly, there are just as many pulpy concepts in the church as there are pulpy words (*see section on Pulpy Wordmanship, above*), many of which can be used to disconcert gatherings of every size and spiritual complexion. Here is another question that has been useful in the past, mainly with groups.[31]

'What feeds us as Christians?'

This is an excellent example, as there appear to be so many possible answers. You will find people suggesting prayer, Bible study, worship, fellowship and forgiveness, to name but a few. Greet each suggestion with that blend of slightly patronizing acceptance and implied dismissal that distinguishes all the worst teachers one has ever known. Finally, when the whole group has run out of plaintive answers and steam and everyone is on the verge of giving up and converting to Islam, propose with calm, confident, fatherly (or motherly) assurance that it would be a good idea to find out what the fourteenth verse of the fourth chapter of the gospel of John has to say on the subject.

Huge relief all round as it is discovered that Christians are fed by – well, for the purposes of this section the answer to the original question is of no interest. Suffice to say that you will be in the position of one who has, as it were, knocked a house down and then rebuilt it to your own design.

---

[31] Needless to say, we are talking in this section about *focussed* questions, the sort that are allowed to have only one answer and are therefore heavily frowned on in training courses for junior teachers.

Other questions for consideration include:

'Who *is* Jesus?' (Select your own preferred option and bat all others away like gnats on a hot summer evening.)

'Is redemption more important than salvation?' (Potentially hours to be wasted on this nonsense.)

'If God asked why you should be allowed through the gates of heaven, what would you say?' (This has a wonderfully paralysing effect.)

'If Jesus was raised from the dead with the marks of the crucifixion on his body, what will happen to people who were crushed in road accidents?' (Offers new life and energy to the bored red herring pursuers.)

'What *is* the church?' (*See section on Tony Bennmanship, below.*)

———————— UNSIGNED GREETING ———————— CARDMANSHIP

In our section on Helpful Tractmanship we have already hinted at the possibilities that exist for those who are willing to utilize modern desktop technology. Here at the College of Churchmanship we have benefited greatly from the wisdom of visiting lecturer Mostyn Deal of Anglesey, who specializes in the design and production of unsigned greeting cards. (*Now available for sale from Churchmanship Headquarters, price fifteen pounds per pack of ten, including postage and packing – please specify design required.*) Our free catalogue of products includes a comprehensive list of Mostyn's designs, but here are three examples (*see illustration*) for members to consider.

(a) Looking forward to your visit!

This brilliantly conceived ploy is designed for use with those Christian speakers who the Churchman or woman deems to be in need of constructive destabilization. (Mark Williams of Cardiff – see section on Sincerity and Churchmanship, above– prefers to use the phrase 'Those gits who are up themselves' but, as we have found it necessary to explain to Mark in the past, the fact that we are engaged in undermining the peace and security of others does not mean that we have to descend into vulgarity. It is the *Christian* church we are not really part of, after all.)

The front of the card announces *Looking Forward to Your Visit!* in a choice of silver or gold lettering, with a cartoon-style illustration of happily smiling people sitting in rows and applauding a speaker who stands behind a lectern on the platform in front of them. Inside, the printed message reads

> For all the joy you soon will bring
> We praise the Lord and dance and sing!

The written message on the opposite side of the card must be given special attention. Mostyn quotes a note that he himself enclosed to the well-known speaker and evangelist who is known, for some strange reason, as 'Bungy'.

Hi, Bunge! Just a quick note to say how much we're all looking forward to you being with us on the nineteenth. Can't believe it's two years since we set this up! I'm so glad I took the risk on this after all the discouragement I got from you-know-who in the early days. Tickets have gone fantastically well – more than four hundred at the last count and still rising. People coming from churches all over the place. Some of the local folks just can't believe that a speaker as well known as you is willing to come to our little neck of the woods. 'Ah, you don't know the man,' I tell them, 'but you mark my words – you will on the nineteenth!' All my best to Beth and Joe and Karen, and not forgetting the two dogs[32] – happy memories, eh?

–W.N.

P.S. Sadly, Gillian is no better, but the prospect of seeing you again in her last days is really helping to keep her going for a little longer.

In the absence of any actual information on the subject, one can only speculate with immense and lingering pleasure on the effect that this communication must have had on the celebrated speaker.

Had he really made some firm arrangement two years ago to go and speak somewhere on the nineteenth? What could have gone so badly wrong with his well-oiled planning machinery? Had he made this arrangement? Had he? Well, *had* he? The nineteenth of what, for goodness' sake? This month? Next month? The month after next? And who on earth or in heaven was W.N.? He didn't know a W.N. And yet it had to be someone he knew because they quoted the names of his wife and children and knew about the dogs. And who

---

[32] An inspiration, this, by Mostyn, who simply lifted the details from Bungy's vast, self-congratulatory tome of a website, and from his amusing and instructive little tales about family life.

was this Gillian? What was the matter with her? What a nightmare! More than four hundred people from lots of churches all sitting in rows waiting expectantly to 'know the man' who had so generously agreed to come to their little neck of the woods!

For at least three or four months Bungy must have racked his brain, desperately trying to conjure up a W.N. from his past as he waited with uneasy dread for the hurt, panic-stricken phone call that was bound to come at some point between seven-thirty and eight o'clock on the evening of the nineteenth of whatever it turned out to be.

Ah, yes, dear Churchman or woman, when the night is dark and the last green bottle is drained and the restless wind howls through the eaves and life itself seems but a hollow sham, these are the reflections that will always lift the spirits of depressed Churchmen and women. Our grateful thanks to Mostyn Deal for his inspirational work.

(b) Wishing you happiness in your retirement

Mostyn designed this attractively depressing collection of greeting cards to be sent to those in their late fifties or early sixties who are still actively and enthusiastically involved in ministry and have no plans to retire in the foreseeable future.

We were particularly taken with the card that depicts a greying, pantalooned, Pilgrim-type figure[33] leaning wearily on his staff at the top of a steep hill as he gazes yearningly down into the valley below where a little country church is surrounded by graves. A narrow shaft of sunlight has pierced the dark and lowering clouds and is brilliantly illuminating one of these graves. The path that winds its way down the hill from the spot where the figure is standing terminates at the entrance to the churchyard. The verse inside the card reads:

> Though eyes grow dim and bones grow sore
> We soon shall sleep for ever more

---

[33] Other designs include single female figures and a tasteful depiction of a male and female couple in an equally crumbling and decrepit state.

Mostyn suggests that the written message need only be brief, and he offers these words as a model.

To dear David and Belinda, as you round that final bend and make your willing but weary way towards the finishing line. Sincere thanks for all that you once were.

—W.N.[34]

(c) Just a reminder!

Yet another flash of brilliance from Mostyn, the front of this card displays the simple message *Just a Reminder!* in the shape of a horseshoe almost circling a champagne cork popping out of a bottle. Inside, the card is blank, but Mostyn suggests a written message of the kind quoted below. (The 'Vaughn' in question, by the way, was Vaughn Day, an international speaker who claimed to regard money as a mere tool but who, as Mostyn put it, was heavily into DIY.)

Vaughn, mate, just a quick note. I haven't heard back from you, but I'm assuming you did get my letter as it was registered and all that. The point is – I gather there's a time limit as far as the gift is concerned, so you do need to get in touch and claim the cash as soon as possible. As I said before I'm not sure of the exact amount within a hundred thousand or so, but the solicitors will fill you in on all that. I'm writing the name and address of the firm of solicitors on this card just in case you've lost it. Be in touch soon, you lucky old devil! Cheers!

—W.N.

Underneath this note Mostyn has written what certainly appears to be a name and address, but the details have been smudged beyond

---

[34] Mostyn always signs himself as 'W.N.' but has never offered a reason for this choice of initials.

recognition by damp or a spillage of some kind. The only information to remain legible is the name of the county, Northumberland.

As a final expensive but utterly inspired touch, Mostyn encloses *a postal order for fifty pounds* and adds a note that reads:

> Hope you won't be offended by this, Vaughn, but the expenses of getting up north and phone calls and all that could get a bit steep, so just in case you're feeling the pinch at present I've popped a bit in to help. You can pay me back when it's all sorted out.

Mostyn writes:

> Just as the poet Wordsworth in pensive mood found his heart filled with pleasure and dancing at the memory of all those tossing daffodils, so I love to picture Vaughn Day (who lives right down on the south coast) frantically attempting to track down every firm of solicitors in the county of Northumberland. By phone first, perhaps, and then, inevitably, by car. Starting in Newcastle probably, and then Gateshead, South Shields, Tynemouth, Morpeth, Ashington and eventually out towards Corbridge, Hexham and other even more far-flung and northerly parts of that huge county (*see illustration*).

'Could be a joke', he will be saying to himself through gritted teeth as he drives furiously around that wonderfully huge county. 'Could be a mistake. Could be a hoax. But fifty pounds! Fifty quid! Why would anyone do that?'

A joy to contemplate. Emotion recollected in tranquillity. That just about sums it up.

——THE STRANGE STRANGER PLOY——

Morton Sayworth of Henfield in Sussex writes to remind us that it is quite possible to successfully disconcert not just an individual, but a whole group of people. Sayworth's Strange Stranger Ploy is highly inventive. Here, in his own words, is a vivid account of the last occasion on which he employed it.

'Our house group was becoming a little too cohesive and serious about their faith for my liking, so I decided to halt the momen-tum by telling them that I was keen on the idea of bringing along a friend of mine who was a "real seeker". The members of my house group always become very keen and animated on those rare occasions when a "real seeker" hoves into view, so they were most encouraging. Accordingly, the very next Thursday I brought along my friend[35] Tony Hyssop who, like most sane people, will do virtually anything for a couple of large Cobras and a curry.

'I had previously shared with the group (we never simply tell each other anything, we always "share" things) that, although a very nice person and a genuine seeker after truth, Tony had one small problem. He suffered from the chronic delusion that a swarm of bees was intent on persecuting him. This problem, I explained, could manifest itself at any time or in any place. I would be most grateful,

---

[35] See section on Off-colour Jokemanship, below, for further reference to the value of importing paid outsiders in the pursuit of excellence in Churchmanship ploys.

in the event of this happening, if the members of the group could find it in their hearts to react as though he was behaving perfectly normally. They earnestly assured me that they would do exactly as I had asked.

'The visit turned out to be a great success from my point of view, although I had perhaps forgotten or slightly underestimated Tony's tendency to overact in these situations. No more than two seconds after entering the sitting room he dipped his body abruptly in a most extraordinary way – bending his knees and swaying his body deftly to one side and his head to the other as if his face had come under attack. The postures of the various group members acquired a certain rigidity on witnessing this, but in all other respects they displayed admirable restraint.

'From that point onward, the "real seeker" appeared to detect the presence of bees everywhere. Just as the Bible study was about to start, for instance, he suddenly dropped to his knees and began a slow-motion crawl across the carpet holding a rolled up newspaper in one hand, his feverish gaze fixed intently on a very mild man called Derek Stephens, who was sitting opposite.

'I must give Derek his due. When he found himself wildly attacked around the head with a rolled-up copy of the *Baptist Times* he managed to pipe out in a high-pitched voice, "Er, thank you! Thank you so much for dealing with the er – the bees! Have – have they all gone now, or are there still some er . . .?"

'Thereafter it was all bees. At one point we had to sit in silence for nearly three minutes while Tony urged us to eavesdrop on a conversation between two bees who were sitting in the chimney plotting his downfall. We all heard them. Well, we all said we did.

'Tony's *pièce de résistance* was truly spectacular. As soon as he had finished his coffee and biscuits, the bees obviously decided to stop messing about and to come for him in a big way. After rushing round and round the room several times beating the air with both hands, he disappeared into the hall and could be heard running up and down the stairs and in and out of the bedrooms at a lunatic rate. When he eventually returned to the sitting room, he grabbed the metal handles of the old sash window, dragged it open and clambered out, screaming loudly as he disappeared into the night, "The bees! Oh, the bees! Misery is manifold![36] The bees are coming! Someone must save me from the bees!"

'Later, in a not so local Indian restaurant, Tony sipped from his second glass of Cobra and asked if his visit had had the effect I was hoping for.

' "Oh, yes," I replied, "we'll probably be talking about you for some time. All in all, I think it's safe to say that your visit caused quite a – what's the word I'm searching for?"

' "Don't say it."

' "All right, I won't. Another Cobra?" '

──────OFF-COLOUR JOKEMANSHIP──────

We are often asked to describe the correct Churchmanship ploy when listening to off-colour jokes told by people in or from the church. The answer to this question revolves around the issue of definition. We as Churchmen and women should be dictating the moral status

---

[36] Sayworth tells us that he has had occasion in the past to warn Tony Hyssop against peppering his performances with absurdly archaic phrases lifted from short stories by Edgar Allan Poe. The ethos we are aiming to create is more 'X-Files' than 'Hammer Horror'..

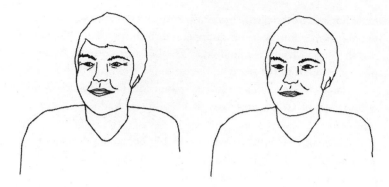

of jokes, not accepting the judgements of others. C. Telfor, once of Glasgow, now ejected (*see also The Notebook Ploy, above*) is an expert in this field and offers valuable advice and elucidation.

'There will be times when it is far more productive to respond to a perfectly clean and respectable joke as though it were utterly disgusting or sacrilegious. I recall, for instance, a church party where a mild, wispy and exceedingly annoying person called Maxwell K. Thornton said he would like to tell me a joke involving a hare, a mushroom and some flower-fairies.

'As usual, I commenced my ploy by adopting an air of tolerant, playful expectancy (*see illustration*), succeeded after thirty seconds or so by the application of my trademark Fading Smile technique, perfected during hours and hours of painstaking practice in front of the mirror at home (*see illustration for stages of fading*). By the time Thornton approached the end of his pathetic but harmless little story I was sitting completely still, staring at him with a totally expressionless face. I maintained this posture in silence throughout the punchline and beyond.

'Thornton became more and more pink and agitated, perhaps surmising that there might be something obscurely perverted or new-age about fairies or hares or mushrooms or an unholy combination of all three. Possibly he was asking himself if my father or some other close relative might have choked to death on a hare bone, or suffered a breakdown after bigots in the neighbourhood had shouted 'Fairy!' at him as he walked through the streets of our town.

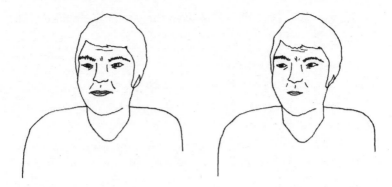

Eventually I simply stood up and moved away without a word. Two days later, I received a note from Thornton apologizing for his behaviour at the party. I totally forgave him, of course, and was extremely gracious and genial in my contacts with him from that day onwards.

'Conversely, there will be times when the correct strategy is to disconcert those who are expressing disapproval of a truly repulsive joke. I once paid a horrible acquaintance of mine called Frank Billings twenty pounds to come to a church event pretending to know no one (especially me) and to tell a dreadful story about General Custer, a mackerel and some Indians. As I had expected, the joke was received with both tight-lipped *and* openly expressed disapproval by three or four of those present. I laughed in a "What the heck does it matter as long as we preach the Gospel?" fashion, put my arm around Frank's shoulders and said, "Don't worry, mate, we don't all judge a man by a few silly words that come out of his mouth. I reckon the joke was genuinely funny, whatever else it may have been. Let's you and me go for a little stroll outside and you can tell me what's going on in your life."

'The next Sunday I paid Billings another twenty pounds to drag himself out of his pit so that he could come to church and sit next to me looking tearfully vulnerable and brightly interested in everything that was going on. After the service I was very, very friendly to those who had disapproved of the mackerel joke, making a point of asking if they had any tips on personal evangelism, as I wasn't sure I'd "got it right with Billings". They looked at the floor, clearly filled with much rue, and said little.'

THE HATTERSLEY HEAVING PLOY

Useful in planning sessions, PCC meetings, and any other assembly where serious debate is being carried out, this ploy is modelled on a specific strategy employed by ex-Labour Cabinet minister Roy Hattersley, who describes himself as an atheist but would, we are surely all agreed, make a fine Churchman.

Hattersley's most dynamic piece of Disconcertmanship occurs when he has already had his (usually considerable) say in a discussion and is subsequently bound by the rules of debate at least to pretend to listen to an opposing argument from the other person. The problem he has so cleverly solved is how to remain actively involved in the debate despite the fact that he is not allowed to say anything. Choosing a moment when his opponent has made a clear point (any old point will do) he will begin to heave and shake with silent but apparently uncontrollable laughter, as though the other person has made a statement so risibly foolish that it deserves to be treated more as entertainment than as serious argument.

The debilitating influence of someone like Hattersley rotundly quivering with hilarity beside you when you are trying to say something you truly believe in should not be underestimated. We Churchmen and women may not all be physically constructed like 'The Tory slayer', but we can be just as successful in our use of his ploy.

TONY BENNMANSHIP

Here is still more useful material gathered from the floor of the Labour stable. Simplicity itself. Establish the nature of a view held by all those in authority and declare yourself passionately in favour of the exact opposite. Always good for a round of applause in public debate, and an 'Amen!', a 'Praise the Lord!' or a selection of sober nods in church circles.

Durham Steadman offers a truly excellent example of Tony Bennmanship as executed by himself in the context of a home group attached to St Mary's Church, Framlingham.

HOUSE GROUP LEADER: (*winding up some earlier remarks*) Having said that, there are areas where we will always be one hundred percent in agreement. For instance, we are committed to the eternal truth that the church is not some weird building just round the corner from Tesco's, but a body of believers meeting to worship God.

STEADMAN: (*trenchantly, and in the tone of one who simply cannot hold his tongue any longer*) Can I be allowed to just say a word about that? You've made a couple of clever remarks about a strange building round the corner from the supermarket. Very entertaining and all that but, you know, to a lot of ordinary people, and I include myself under that heading, that 'weird' building, as you mockingly call it, is actually a solid symbol of faith in our town. Go down to this supermarket of yours and just ask Mr or Mrs uncommitted average shopper where they think the church is. They'll tell you exactly where it is. If you ask me, we should be making sure that *the* 'church' is happening up there *in* the church, if you take my meaning. I don't know what anyone else thinks, but I've got a feeling theological niceties have to give way to practical Christianity from time to time.[37] (*nods and murmurs of agreement all round*)

HOUSE GROUP LEADER: Er, well, yes of course . . .

---

[37] Amazingly, the logical vacuum within this foolish remark went completely unnoticed.

THE PATRONIZING PATRICIA PLOY

Another rich source of material for the dedicated churchwoman, this ploy is based on the extraordinarily annoying verbal delivery of the Right Honourable Patricia Hewitt, Labour Member of Parliament for Leicester West, and at one time Secretary of State for Health. Miss Hewitt addresses individuals and groups alike as though she is the deputy head of a small private school telling 4B off because, in the course of an educational excursion, they have let down, not just her and their parents, but more importantly themselves, by making rude signs at passers-by through the windows of the school bus. Hewitt's maddeningly measured, slow motion, pile-driving style of speech is so stupefyingly patronizing and inaccessible to argument that listeners are reduced to an open-mouthed, impotent fury of disbelief that anyone could speak to another human being in such a way.

We are well aware that students and members might wish to point out that such an unsubtle ploy is not suited to the serious business of Churchmanship. We understand this concern, but we would ask them to bear in mind the enigma of ex-Prime Minister Margaret Thatcher. Despite her delivery being Hewitt to the power of ten, Thatcher was able to hang on to leadership for a surprisingly long period. Why was this? Largely, we would suggest, because a majority of the populace seemed to hear the voice of their junior school headmistress when she spoke. Automatically and weakly, they assumed that, however unpleasant further acquaintance with the woman would undoubtedly be, she must surely turn out to be right in the end.

Many church congregations and groups are similarly vulnerable to the voice of confident certainty, however ghastly the sound of that voice might be, and we do hope you will give consideration to this ploy.

In support of our recommendation we can report that June Osborne of Swissgate Christian Centre in Eastbourne once stood up at the front of the church minibus in the course of a trip to some theatre event in London, and gave a 'good telling off' to the Deputy Mayor of Eastbourne when he began to open his sandwich packet before all the others. The man coloured heavily and hastily rewrapped his picnic, hardly daring to so much as look at it again until half an hour later, when June briskly announced that *now* was the time for everyone to start. Need we say more? Gain control. Try this ploy.

Section 12
GIVING HEARTMANSHIP

It is, of course, an unwritten principle of Churchmanship that Churchmen and women will never give away time, money or attention unless there is a clear and strategic reason for doing so. Nor do we wish to emulate the foolishness of the infamous Scotsman who gave away millions in order to conceal his stinginess. On the other hand, it is essential that we appear to be overflowing with the spirit of generosity. No one has done finer work in this area than Gilbert Payne, once entombed in Ruislip but now firmly established at the New Life Fellowship in Streatham where he is held up to the youth of the church as a shining example of open-handedness and good stewardship. This is a remarkable achievement by one of the meanest, most narrow-spirited and selfish men I have ever known. For that reason his ploys are bound to repay study.

————— NO HOLIDAYS FOR————— ME-MANSHIP

Gilbert's idea of a good holiday has been consistent and unvarying for the last twenty years. As he himself puts it, 'Sit me under a parasol by a pool in a hot country with a large gin and tonic in one hand and a fat anthology of locked room mysteries in the other and I'll be happy. Make sure there's a four-course meal and an air-conditioned room in a five-star hotel waiting for me every night, and that'll be little Gilbert well-suited for a fortnight.'

When asked by members of his church where it was that he had so mysteriously disappeared to at holiday times during his first couple of years at Streatham, Gilbert appeared shyly reluctant to answer at first. When pressed, however (Gilbert Payne was able to provoke and manipulate other people into 'pressing him' with greater skill and subtlety than any other Churchman I have known), he haltingly replied:

'Oh, well, if you must know, there's a project thingy near where I used to live up Ruislip way. It's a place that offers a bit of a leg up to fellers and ladies who are, you know, down on their luck for one reason or another. I don't know about holidays and all that sort of thing, but I do know that the team down there are always needing a bit of a helping hand from folks who've got time and energy to give away, so – well . . .'

At this point Gilbert would scuff the path roughly with the toe of his shoe and glare with fierce embarrassment into the distance before continuing.

'Quite honestly, what I do for them during that fortnight amounts to nothing – nothing at all.'

He was speaking the exact truth. He did nothing at all for them during his fortnight's holiday. There was such a charity next to the Salvation Army Citadel in Denham Road near Ruislip Railway Station, and Gilbert's contribution to their work did indeed amount to precisely nothing. He had never once been there. Impressed by Gilbert's sacrificial giving of his leisure time, some church members insisted on offering donations to 'the work'. Gilbert always declined twice before accepting, and thanked the giver gravely, promising that all contributions would be used to provide food, drink and useful literature where those commodities would be most urgently needed and appreciated. He was as good as his word. A constant supply of G&Ts, four-course meals and detective novels does not come cheap.

GIVING TO A GOOD CAUSEMANSHIP

Preparation is everything. Whenever Gilbert Payne knew that a collection was likely to be made in church for some cause or other, he would empty the pot in which he collected brown change for just such an eventuality and fill both of his trouser pockets. He always added a peppering of silver, at least two crumpled five-pound notes and some vague scraps of paper with bits of red and green or blue (scribbled on in advance with crayons by Payne) that might possibly be currency notes, but were actually not.[38]

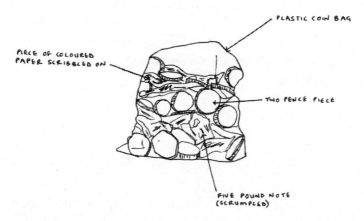

PLASTIC COIN BAG

PIECE OF COLOURED PAPER SCRIBBLED ON

TWO PENCE PIECE

FIVE POUND NOTE (SCRUMPLED)

I have personally witnessed Payne's execution of this ploy at his church in Streatham. It was a Sunday when the service revolved around a charity engaged in helping homeless children in Latin America. At the end of the service Payne approached two people

---

[38] Under some pressure from those of us whose knowledge of incriminating information is matched only by our strong spirit of conditional discretion, Gilbert Payne has kindly agreed to allow us full franchise rights in this ploy. We are therefore now able to offer our members specially prepared packets of coins and notes to be used in collections of this kind (*available from Churchmanship Headquarters, price fifteen pounds including postage and packing – see illustration*).

at the door who were collecting in metal buckets for the cause, took a handful of change from his pocket, and started sorting through it with one finger as if trying to decide how much to give. Then, with a rueful smile and a little shake of the head (masterful, both of these), he said, 'Good heavens, it's for the kiddies. Go on with you – you might as well have the lot.'

Having tipped his whole handful of change into one of the buckets, he then emptied the entire contents of both his pockets into the other. The echoing cascade of coins and what appeared to be several notes was truly impressive. There was no doubt about it. Those who dropped discreetly folded cheques for ten times the amount Payne had given, or who committed themselves to monthly payments of twenty pounds for the next fifteen years, appeared miserably mean and penny pinching in comparison.

The lesson we learn from Gilbert Payne in this ploy is clear. Give your all with publicly extravagant open-handedness, but make sure you only bring a bit of your all with you.[39]

A small investment for a significant return.

It is worth mentioning that Payne had already made quite an impact in this area when he walked out of a hunger lunch that had been organized by the church to raise money for Third World projects. The lunch itself consisted of thin vegetable soup and a rather boring bread roll. Payne took one mouthful of the insipid soup then dropped his spoon with a clatter on the table and, rising to his feet, addressed the assembly in a voice that suggested he was in severe emotional pain.

'I begin to be sickened by all this food and drink,' he cried. 'This is not a hunger lunch. This is a feast. I am inwardly rebuked and accused by serried ranks of staring, hungry eyes and swollen bellies. I cannot eat another mouthful in this place.'

---

[39] For all we know, the widow who gave her mite in the New Testament was awash with mites back at home but had wisely decided to only bring one out with her. An early Churchwoman?

Payne marched out of the hall with quiet, injured dignity, but the staring, hungry eyes and swollen bellies had clearly lost their rebuking and accusing power by the time he reached a different place. Comfortably ensconced by the fire in the saloon bar of the Gardener's Arms out at Cawston Brook half an hour later, he settled down with untroubled enthusiasm to steak and kidney pudding with half a bottle of claret, and apple and raspberry crumble in a veritable pond of custard.

───── THE CHURCH PICNIC PLOY ─────

Nobody here at Churchmanship Headquarters would wish to deny the obvious truth that church picnics are ghastly affairs, rancidly saturated with oleaginous community interaction and saggily relaxed bonhomie. It is good, in view of this frank acknowledgement, to discover from the work of experts such as Gilbert Payne that there are benefits to be gained by the keen Churchman or woman even in this context. Pursuing the theme of public generosity, students would be well advised to study, emulate and adapt his ploy in this area.

Payne would deliberately arrive a little late at church picnics carrying a large, very old, verminous-looking cloth bag. With his shirt hanging out at the back, red-faced and puffed with the effort of walking all the way from his house to the venue despite having a perfectly good car, he would wave at everyone with a nicely pitched, plaintive good humour and greet all enquiries as to why he hadn't driven or phoned someone for a lift with, 'Bless you, no, it's only a step.'

He would then plump himself down on the grass in an endearingly flustered way and take out his contribution to the picnic. This invariably consisted of loads of crumbling cakes and biscuits and rolls of varying shapes and sizes jammed unappetizingly together in a set of ancient cake tins that were just beginning to rust with age. Payne then circulated the whole picnic, insisting with great gusto and a touchingly pathetic cheeriness that people take as much as they wanted, saying things like, 'Come on, dig in to my prog.[40] Take two or three, it's all got to go.'

And indeed it did all have to go. As soon as possible. Payne's dreadful food was out of date stuff that he had managed to beg for nothing from the local baker two days before, late on the Friday evening. It was horribly stale and crumbled to fragments in your hand as soon as you took hold of it. A weevil was once discovered by a child.

Of course, everyone pretended to be grateful, hiding their crumbs under their blankets and in their pockets or digging little holes in the ground to put it in, and offering Payne all sorts of really good stuff like wine and fruit and freshly made sandwiches in return.[41]

Remarkably, Payne ate and drank everyone else's food and drink but still managed to appear the generous author of the feast – all without spending a penny.

Pure Churchmanship.

---

[40] Prog? What is it about the cheery use of terms defunct since schoolboys used them in 1949 that is so deeply annoying?

[41] Gilbert Payne's skill in obtaining free meals and invitations to dinner is legendary in Churchmanship circles. One of his favourite and most productive ploys was to talk loudly about 'us sad old singletons who live on baked beans and a scrap of toast'. Few were aware that Payne lived next door to his sister, a very accomplished cordon bleu cook who regularly tested all of her most accomplished recipes on her brother.

Appendix

QUESTIONS SELECTED, EDITED AND ANSWERED BY PROFESSOR PETER CAWS

Continual requests from students and members have persuaded me that a question and answer section should appear in every annual report from this year onwards. Questions for this feature in next year's report should be addressed to me, Professor Peter Caws, at Churchmanship House, Broad Road, Great Malvern, WD 40. Each year I shall select the most representative of these questions and attempt to provide constructive answers.

Dear Professor Caws,

I have got myself involved with a group of itinerant Christian speakers who go away together two or three times each year in order to '*offer one another prayerful support and assistance in a ministry that is common to all of us*'. Of course, despite having a full diary of preaching engagements I have no genuine ministry as such, but the excessive eating and drinking is always a pleasure, and – let us be honest – these evangelists and speakers may not be accredited Churchmen, but they have an awful lot to teach us. My problem is this. One element of the evening and morning that we spend together is an opportunity to share deep personal needs and receive prayer in that area from the other members of the group. Naturally there is no question of my sharing anything of any real importance, but how do I deal with this dismal and, frankly, pointless interruption to all the eating and drinking?

–Puzzled of Caterham

Dear Puzzled,

First of all, let me assure you that you will not be the only member of that little assembly who is failing to share genuine personal problems. It is a characteristic of such groups that a great deal of hot air (evangelists, remember) is spoken about everybody being really open and honest about what is happening in their private lives. Almost nobody is. You cannot prescribe intimacy – a fact which might well destroy the evangelical church if it ever becomes common knowledge. However, some are more adept at pretending to do so than others.

I used to belong to a similar group known as GLUMBISCUIT, a pleasantly cumbrous acronym of God Loves Us Madly But I Sin Continually Under Intense Temptation. As a matter of fact, for purely strategic reasons I ran the GLUMBISCUITS for several years and therefore was faced with the problem that you describe every four months or so for quite a long time. Here is my advice to you. The secret lies in (a) coming up with some personal dilemma that will cause you to be seen in a good light whichever way it is resolved, but even more importantly in (b) expressing that dilemma with such anguish as to appease the gobblers of spiritual carrion who will no doubt be perched on a nearby branch or hovering restlessly around you.

I remember one afternoon with the GLUMBISCUITS, for example, when I confessed (with a tremor in my voice that was beautifully judged, though I say it myself) that I was torn between donating a percentage of my capital to international aid relief and giving the money to a selection of local charities based in my own town. What a dilemma! I explained to the rest of the group that I had been unable to sleep for the last week as I wrestled with a growing conviction that the Lord was calling me to give to other countries, and not to needy folk in the town that I loved.

'It's so very tough,' I explained brokenly, 'to face up to the need for obedience instead of simply doing what I want as usual. It's all about me, I'm afraid. Pure selfishness. I want to be good, but – well, you fellows know what I'm talking about, don't you?'

Oh, they did, they really did, and they were deeply sympathetic to my desperate, pain-filled plight. After a few quiet, respectful questions they prayed me through to the place of obedience and, accordingly, on Wednesday afternoon of the next week I told the lady at Oxfam to keep the thirty-five pence change that I was owed after buying a birthday present for my mother.

Mind you, there never was any question of giving locally. The scene on market day in my town makes Hieronymus Bosch look like Beatrix Potter. Those stumbling, Brueghelesque gargoyles are not squeezing any thirty-five pences out of me.

Incidentally, after the incident described above I took the opportunity later in the afternoon to gently express my concern to the group that people were not being as open and vulnerable in their requests for prayer as we might have hoped and expected. After all, I went on to say firmly but kindly, every one of us had made an agreement that we wouldn't hold anything back, and as brothers in faith we must try not to let each other down.

My little speech had quite an effect. Norman Buddley said that my vulnerability in asking for prayer about my dilemma over giving earlier in the afternoon had greatly inspired him, and he went on to confess to something so virulently unpleasant and distasteful that it would have come close to putting me off my dinner if it wasn't for the fact that nothing puts me off my dinner.

Hope this helps.

–Peter Caws

Dear Sir,

Since graduating from Great Malvern two years ago I have been generally happy with my progress as a Churchman in the field, except in the area of extemporary prayer. At present I am in danger of becoming tongue-tied and, dare I say, sincere at every meeting I attend. Could you suggest a subject or list of subjects that would be appropriate in this context?

   –Jack of Herts

Dear Jack,
   I can tell you with absolute confidence that, church communities being as they are, there is almost no subject on earth that cannot be used as the basis for extemporary prayer. For a short time I belonged to a house church near Bexley Heath which happened to be also attended by Charlie Peach, my old roomie from our days at Frome. Finding ourselves attached to the same Bible-study group, Charlie and I would sometimes amuse ourselves by playing a secret game when it came to the prayer time. This consisted of exchanging slips of paper on which we had written 'challenging' topics for prayer. Only rarely did either of us fail to meet these challenges. Between us over the period of a year or so we successfully tackled such diverse subjects as curry, cloud formations, elephants, Charles Dickens, isotopes, personal pronouns and Gillingham Football Club.
   I thought I might have finally stumped Charlie on the evening when I passed him a sheet from my little notebook bearing the legend 'curved reflective surfaces'. How wrong can you be? I should never have doubted the power and ingenuity of such a skilled practitioner. Charlie delivered his prayer on the subject with a totally convincing and beautifully judged blend of soupiness and driving, monotonous intensity. There might have been an air of slight puzzlement emanating from the rest of the group as he began, but within a very short time they were driving along with him. This was his prayer.

   Lord, we thank you for curved reflective surfaces. We thank you for those surfaces and, Lord, we know, Lord, that they are curved. Lord, they are reflective. We thank you, Lord, that those surfaces are not flat, and they are not the kind of surfaces, Lord, that do not reflect. They do reflect, Lord, and yet, Lord, because of the curve, Lord, Lord, that reflection is a distorted one, Lord. Lord, we know that our reflection in you, Lord, is not a distorted one. Lord, it is clear. Thank you for that clearness, Lord, Lord, for that clarity. Lord, you are not that curved reflective surface that does not reflect us in a clear way, Lord, and we thank you that, Lord, we can learn from those curved reflected surfaces that, Lord, you have set in our path. Lord, may we understand and know, Lord, the clearness, Lord, the clarity of our reflection in you, Lord. Lord, bless all surfaces that are curved and reflected to our use, Lord, we pray. Amen.

Take heart, Jack. Why not start with something easy like Velcro or Trafalgar Square and work your way up from there? Good luck!

—Peter Caws

Dear Sir,

I belong to a Christian reading group attached to my church. Once a month we meet to discuss books that people have found improving or helpful. Most of these books have about as much edge as a fresh jam doughnut. I have been watching carefully for opportunities to use principles of Churchmanship in this situation, but so far all I have managed to do is create a slight *frisson* with my contention that small children should be shielded from contact with those who disapprove of Harry Potter books. Have you any suggestions for additional ploys?

—Marlon of Wigan

Dear Marlon,

I have consulted with those more accustomed to this area of work, and they suggest one or two ideas that might be worth trying. Bear in mind, however, that the use of ploy (1) would necessarily preclude the use of ploys (2) and (3)

(1) Take a substantial Bible along with you to the group, raise it above your head at a point when there has been animated talk about purely secular literature, and say, in the ringing tones of one who has heard the trumpet sound and is ready to march alone behind the banner if necessary, 'Would someone like to tell me clearly and without equivocation[42] just one good, solid reason why we should bother with any other book than this?'

(2) Boldly suggest that a book like *Silence of the Lambs* is more truly a spiritual book than any found in Christian bookshops, dealing as it does with the dissolution of a human life, stark issues of good and evil and the power and relevance of personal morality. Ask the other members of the group if they genuinely wish to grapple with the real world, as Jesus did, or simply hide in the Christian ghetto, refusing to raise their eyes from limp and meaningless pap that merely makes them feel safe.

(3) Perhaps cashing in on a successful execution of ploy (2), tell the group that you have discovered a work of fiction that upholds all the finest traditions of literature, and that they are bound to find it constructive and uplifting. On the other hand, you will point out, the section you are about to read contains a number of swear words they would certainly find unacceptable, and therefore you have replaced them with stars corresponding to the number of letters used in each of the offending words. My good friend and colleague Darley Jameson has kindly e-mailed a helpful extract, read by him one afternoon last year at a group in Whitstable that calls itself the 'Ladies' and Gentlemen's Lovely Literature Hour'.

'Six star me!' exclaimed Russell to himself as he opened the front door to admit Peers. 'Why the four star did I ever get involved with this seven star little eight star?'

---

[42] For goodness' sake practice this word before you use it.

Standing in the narrow hall a few seconds later the two men stared at each other for a silent moment, both aware that their relationship was about to end.

'Right', said Russell at last in hard, chilled tones, 'I've only got one thing to say to a stupid six star like you. You've four starred me around ever since I had the seven star, six star misfortune to get involved with you and your constant four star, you six star little pile of five star. I mean, for four star's sake! I'm seven starred if I understand why I should be expected to sort out every six star problem you encounter, you four star-faced eight star four starrer. Everything you say is a load of seven stars, and from now on I'm not six star involved, you seven star, six star, eight star of a seven star little four star. Do I make myself seven star clear? Four star off!'

As the door slammed Russell turned and gazed at his reflection in the hall mirror.

'Oh, four star!' he exclaimed, 'He really is an eight star, but I hope I got it right.'

Hope these ploys work. Just do your seven star best.

−Peter Caws

Dear Sir,

There is a man in my house group who is causing me problems. He is one of those older men with a full head of well-organized white hair, strikingly symmetrical socks and a disturbing blend of amiability and insightful authority. Recently he has been coming over to sit with me at coffee time. He fixes me with his eye and asks me how things are going 'on the spiritual side'. I feel like a moth pinned against a board and I never know what to say. My great fear is that I could be drawn into some gruesomely sincere expression of my feelings which, I need hardly add, would be the thin end of a very unwelcome wedge for a conscientious Churchman such as myself. Any suggestions?

—Earl of Northampton

Dear Earl (I take it you are a man called Earl who lives in Northampton as opposed to an aristocrat with his seat in the midlands),

I once encountered precisely the problem you mention, and from a man (his name was Denis) so startlingly similar to the one you describe that I find myself wondering if there could be some college or institution that specializes in turning out white-haired, insightful persons of this type. The ploy I used took a most satisfactory course, but I should emphasize the need to pace oneself inwardly. There must be no panic. Insight must be countered with (apparently) even greater insight.

> DENIS: (*seeming to peer intently into my soul*) So, Peter, my old mate, how are things going – faith-wise, I mean?
>
> ME: (*slowly and meaningfully, after a long pause during which I seem to peer with equal intensity into his soul*) Denis, have you ever thought of training to be a counsellor?
>
> DENIS: Er, well . . .
>
> ME: I think you should. In my heart I really think you should.
>
> DENIS: It's not something I've thought of.
>
> ME: You have the gift, Denis. (*prodding the air with my finger in the direction of his eyes*) You see into people. You see into their souls. You are gifted. Nurture your gift.
>
> DENIS: My gift.
>
> ME: Yes. Nurture it. May I say something to you, Denis?
>
> DENIS: Er, yes, of course . . .
>
> ME: What I see in you tonight, Denis, is confirmation of something I've sensed and felt for some time.

DENIS: Is it?

ME: (*miming helpfully*) Take your gift in both hands, Denis. Hold it lovingly like a helpless, bedraggled little baby bird. Feed it and nurture it. One day it will become beautiful and (*locking my thumbs together and miming the flight*) then it will fly. Give your gifting wings, Denis. (*standing to go, nodding gently and smiling serenely as though a divine plan has at last been accomplished*) Bless you, Denis, in all that you do, mate.

DENIS: Er, right, yes. Thanks . . .

That was the end of Denis fixing me with his eye. In fact, he seemed to avoid contact with me after that evening. I think he might have felt a little guilty about failing to nurture his gift. I can't be sure, though, as I have very little insight into these matters. Good luck with your white-haired man, Earl. May slightly odd socks crown your efforts.

–Peter Caws

Dear Sir,

I am well aware that competent students and practitioners of Churchmanship will never express open aggression or hostility in their dealings with others (unless, of course, there is some very good strategic reason for doing so). Are you able to suggest or describe a ploy that allows insults to be delivered in a fulsomely polite manner, especially in the context of debate and disagreement?

–Craig of Upper Dicker

Dear Craig,

I understand your problem, and I would advise you to spend some time studying a ploy that won first prize in our annual Velvet Glove competition last year. Developed and refined by the superbly named Hamlet Gunnel of Ipswich, it is tellingly entitled *The Art of Aggressive Apology.* As the great Darley Jameson pithily remarked when he was keynote speaker at our international conference two months ago:

> If, in debate of any kind, a person precedes their point with any expression of apology, you may safely assume that you are dealing with a conscious or unconscious Churchman or woman. Prepare to be manipulated at best, and insulted at worst.

Jameson is, of course, absolutely right in his assertion, and it is essential that the keen Churchman or woman be both warned against and armed with this invaluable weapon in its variety of forms. The capacity for insulting by the use of gracious words is at the very core of all we do. Examples of aggressive apology suggested by Hamlet Gunnel in his prize-winning ploy are listed below in commonly employed contexts, each accompanied by the actual meaning of the sentence. (*Full list available from Churchmanship Headquarters, price three pounds including postage and packing.*)

(a) I'm sorry, but I simply cannot see my way to agreeing with what you say.
   (*I'm not sorry, and you're an idiot.*)
(b) Forgive me, but I'm having real problems with accepting that point of view.
   (*Your forgiveness is the last thing I want, especially bearing in mind that I haven't done anything wrong and you're an idiot.*)
(c) Pardon me, but I'm getting just a little confused about this.
   (*What I am completely clear about is the blindingly obvious fact that you're an idiot.*)
(d) With all due respect, I fail to see the validity of that way of thinking.
   (*In your case, all due respect means precisely – let me see, er – none, you being wrong and an idiot.*)

(e) Help me to understand the direction you're coming from with this.[43]

(*You are a dumbo-brained, thick-headed idiot.*)

I do hope that you will avail yourself of Hamlet's complete list accompanied by operating instructions, and that this will enable you to add a useful dimension of warmth and courtesy to your fundamental and necessary unpleasantness.

—Peter Caws

---

[43] Hamlet has asked me to state that he is deeply indebted to P. MacCusker of Colorado Springs for this fine addition to his list, involving as it does such an expertly buried layer of False Humilitymanship, a ploy that has been famously perfected over recent years in MacCusker's place of work, a Christian institution built on a promontory above the city in an area known by local people as 'Moral Heights'

So there we are. That is the document given to me by Peter Caws, and what an extraordinary piece of work it is. You will draw your own conclusions and examine your own responses, but let me tell you how it has affected me. I have become uneasy – not just about my own hidden agenda, but about the motivations of others.

Last Sunday, for instance, Walter Ovenden, a much respected older member of our church, came up to me at coffee time after the morning service and made the following statement with what seemed to me to be studied casualness.

'I thought you might like to know I've decided that the time has probably come for me to step down from my role as coordinator of the stewarding. It has given me great joy over the last few years, but I would like to give someone else the chance to be as blessed as I have been.'

I stared at him for a moment, filled with suspicion by his use of the phrase Step Down. Had I discovered a secret exponent of Churchmanship? Was it possible that Ovenden had studied under Professor Peter Caws?

'Good heavens, no, Walt,' I replied lightly. 'I'm absolutely confident that everyone would much rather you continued to experience all that joy and blessing for a good long time to come. You be a little bit selfish, old man, and carry on indulging yourself.'

Did I detect a tightening of the mouth and a flicker of anger in Ovenden's eyes as he listened to this speech? Was it accompanied by just the hint of a question? Might he have been asking himself if his roots and mine had been planted in the same rarefied soil?

'Well,' he said with a beautifully judged, bluff solemnity, 'it's all as the Lord leads, isn't it?'

I tucked my bottom lip between my teeth and nodded diagonally. Inwardly, I thought, 'Ah, yes, Plan B. The Leading of the Lord. Good one, Walt.'

Later, at home, I stared at my reflection in the hall mirror. Walter may or may not be one of Caws' students, I told myself, but what about me? What could I see in my own face – in my own life? To what extent might I be an unconscious Churchman, just like old Byron Marnott?

It is unlikely that I shall find a simple answer to that question, but it seems quite important to go on asking. Don't you agree?